The Ugly Mouths of America!

Neal Crosier

Contents

I want to thank several people who have been very inspirational in my life. As always, I need to start with my lovely wife of twenty-six years, Minetta. You have always been a source of encouragement, putting your trust in me at times when I could barely trust myself. Both spiritually and physically, your love has proven to be a continuous bond for our family. For our precious moments together and the small things that you've done and continue to do that may seem to go unnoticed, I want to say thank you. I love you!

To Will, my exceptional, caring, and giving brother and a great family man: I want to thank you for assisting Dad in helping me to develop into the man that I have become. I sure wish Dad could have been here to see the first black president of the United States.

To my sister, Lynda: you were used by our loving Creator to introduce me to his inspired word, the Bible. This has led to many years of spiritual development and a host of blessings, including my wife and a spiritual family the world over. Thank you!

To Mother: well, what can you say about a mother's love? I thank you for a lifetime of support, development, sacrifice, and care, all of which you have so lovingly provided. May the true God continue to bless you with good health and many more years of life.

To my nieces, nephews, and all the family: much love.

Finally, to my lifelong friends, William W., Kevin T., David (Dee), Bobbie D., and so many others that I cannot name you all, but you know who you are: thanks for your friendship.

And to everyone else: thank you. Now please read my book!

Introduction: An Ugly Mouth!

First and foremost, in calling my book *The Ugly Mouths of America!* my intent is not to judge the individuals described within this publication. I am only recognizing and acknowledging the simple fact that the vast majority of the messages these people present and broadcast daily, whether good or bad, are in opposition to those held by the powers currently governing our country.

In the past, the terms "loudmouth," "trash-talker," and "talking head," among others, has been used to refer to an extreme and outspoken individual. I choose to refer to these kinds of people as "ugly mouths" both because of the contents of their messages and, most importantly, because of the deep-seated attitude out of which their views arise and the spirit in which their messages are delivered.

Taken together, their messages amount to a new movement with an attitude that claims to center around the motives and objectives of our nation's founding fathers. Some call it mainstream conservativeness; others say it is objectionable, prejudice, racist, abusive, derogatory, defamatory, harassing, divisive, vulgar, threatening, and offensive. Put simply, some say it is just plain hate speech. Without a doubt, these messages contribute to a division among our people in this great nation. Positive or negative, good or bad, it presents an alarming issue in need of concern.

Rush Limbaugh, who calls his network the EIB (Excellence In Broadcasting) Network and says he is "America's anchorman," has, according to the *Washington Post* (2009),[1] a listening audience of roughly 14.2 to 25 million people (on average, 19.6 million).Mr. Limbaugh is primarily known for his outrageous and racially charged comments. For example, he was quoted by *Media Matters of America* as saying that President Obama is "more African in his roots than he is American" and is "behaving like an African colonial despot."[2] In reference to another famous Afro-American, he stated, "[Obama] wouldn't have been

3

voted president if he weren't black." Then after eluding to Oprah Winfrey, Mr. Limbaugh continued, "There's a lot of guilt out there, show we're not racists, we'll make this person wealthy and big and famous and so forth...If Obama weren't black he'd be a tour guide in Honolulu, or he'd be teaching Saul Alinsky constitutional law or lecturing on it in Chicago."[3] Rush Limbaugh is a popular and famous person of wealth. He boasts "that he is the most trusted man in America." His annual income is about $38 million, and he signed an eight-year contract for $400 million in 2008. As reported by *Business Insider*[4] that contract also included a signing bonus of $100 million. That's a lot of money!

Sean Hannity, a self-proclaimed "great American," calls his mission "the Hannitization of America "(*CBS News*, May 23, 2004). Hannity notes, "I was born to argue...I don't know why. I mean, from arguing with my teachers and, on occasions, my parents, I think I've mastered the art of argument at a fairly young age."[5] Hannity's radio audience is about fifteen million listeners per week, and he is carried by over five hundred stations. His television program draws nearly two and a half million viewers per show. And his annual income? The *Wall Street Journal* reported in July 2008 that Sean Hannity signed a $100 million contract for five years for his radio show.[6] Maybe that's what he means when he calls himself a "great American." Mr. Hannity may think that his popularity and riches has made him great. Being an author of several best-selling books, maybe this too adds to his arrogance. Is he really Hannitizing America? If so, I wonder what exactly does that mean? Does Hannitizing America mean that he wants other to proclaim him as great, or does he want everyone to share his views or opinions on everything?

Glenn Beck, who calls his *Glenn Beck Program* "the fusion of entertainment and enlightenment," was once consumed by alcoholism and abusive drugs. In his keynote address at CPAC in February 2010, he stated, "What's the difference between a communist or socialist and a progressive? Revolution or evolution? One requires a gun and the other eats away slowly."[7] Mr. Beck, a devoted

4

Mormon, often mentions God or refers to the Bible in his radio broadcasts in an attempt to give his views more authority. Yet here is a man who reportedly once fired his assistant for handing him the wrong type of pen.[8] I wonder if that's something Jesus Christ would have done? Beck was quoted in *Forbes* as saying, "I could give a flying crap about the political process...We're an entertainment company."[9] Reportedly, he receives $13 million a year from print, $10 million from radio, $4 million from digital, about $3 million from speaking events, and about $2 million from television programs. That totals to a whopping $32 million per year, which makes for an average of $615,384 per week. As *Forbes* put it, "Beck is crying all the way to the bank"![10] I might add that all of these revenues are from before he started his own syndicated pay-per-view Internet network, Glenn Beck TV (GBTV.com).

Dr. Laura Schlessinger, who has been referred to as the Dragon Lady of talk radio[11] and the female Rush Limbaugh, was the #1 female radio talk show host in the nation. Dr. Schlessinger announced her departure from her radio program after using the word "nigger" on her program on August 10, 2010. During a call with an African-American woman who was seeking advice on how to deal with racist comments from her white husband's friends and relatives, Schlessinger used the word eleven times in less than five minutes. She went on to tell the caller, "Don't take things out of context. Don't double N—NAACP me...If you're that hypersensitive about color and don't have a sense of humor, don't marry out of your race."[12] Dr. Schlessinger's website states that "Dr. Laura Schlessinger offers no-nonsense advice infused with a strong sense of ethics, accountability, and personal responsibility; she's been doing it successfully for more than 30 years, reaching approximately 9 million listeners weekly."[13] She is the author of several self-help books, one of which is entitled *Ten Stupid Things Women Do to Mess up Their Lives.* Maybe she could have helped herself by noting one more stupid thing. In the case of Dr. Schlessinger, and this applies to all, we should think before we speak.

After about two years of listening to Rush Limbaugh, Sean Hannity, Glenn Beck, and sometimes Mark Levine and others, I decided to write about these relentless and outspoken individuals. I wanted to know who these people were and why they were so popular. I wanted a behind-the-scene look that would help me begin to grasp their personalities and ways of thinking and to develop a real feel for their motives and the true driving forces behind what they do. I have to admit that, at the time of writing, I have not met any of these people, although I would like to do so. In fact, when this book is published, I promise to send each of them a free copy. The reason for wanting to meet them is neither because I admire them nor because I despise them, but because I really want to know what makes them tick. Three good indicators of what a person is all about are what they say ("Out of the abundance of the heart, the mouth speaks" [Luke 6:45]), how they act ("Faith without works is dead" [James 2:26]), and to which people and organizations they adjoin themselves ("Bad association spoils useful habits" [1 Corinthians 15:33]).

You may observe that I, like Glenn Beck, choose to back some of my comments in this publication with Biblical text references. Mr. Beck confesses to follow the Mormon religious teachings, which are pulled from both the Bible and the Book of Mormon. I confess to being a Christian, that is, one who follows Christ's teachings and is a student of only the Bible. Neither of us is perfect.

As a Christian, I try to follow the Bible and apply its principles to my everyday living. It is my opinion that the Bible is the finest and the greatest book ever written and that when its principles are properly understood and practiced, they prove to be of great benefit to all mankind. With that said, this book is not a religious one. However, I chose to cite scripture as needed to give the reader a better understanding of the viewpoints I express.

Around the same time I was listening to Rush and his peers, I observed the growth of the modern so-called conservative group known as the **Tea Party**. This

6

organization was rapidly spreading across America. I remember hearing of it while listening to Sean Hannity just a few months after the election of President Obama in 2008. Shortly thereafter, the other UMAs (Ugly Mouths of America) were also promoting this movement.

In July 2010, the **NAACP** (National Association for the Advancement of Colored People), an organization with over ninety years of history of promoting peace, passed a resolution condemning what it called "racist elements within the Tea Party movement."[14] With both negative opposition and positive rapid growth, this fast-moving Tea Party organization was not only on the move—it also demanded my attention.

It's important to note at this time that I have always been neutral to political affairs. Yes, I am a black or Afro-American male, born in Chicago, Illinois, and a natural US citizen. Although President **Barack H. Obama** once lived in Chicago and was a former Illinois Senator, I did not vote for him in 2008. Neither did I vote for anyone else during that election. I will explain in great detail my position and reasoning behind being politically neutral later in chapter 6, "A House Divided." However, it is worth noting now that it was my need to know and my position of neutrality that led me to tune into conservative talk programs and to research these popular hosts as well as to investigate the new Tea Party movement.

The election of a new president who is of at least 50 percent Afro-American descent and has the appearance and statue of a black man was definitely new. America as we knew it was changing. In fact, President Obama had run his victorious campaign for the presidency with the themes of change and hope. The crash of the housing market, economic turmoil, two ongoing wars, unemployment, and a government that no longer had the trust of its people had brought about this need for change. Like it or not, at the completion of George W. Bush's second term in office, the timing was right for Obama. A change has definitely come to America's politics. Now there was a shifting to a democratic

7

administration with a relatively inexperience black man as president. But the question remains: does his administration bring the change and hope that the American public needs and desires?

People respond to change in various ways. I can recall a motivational speaker once explaining how people react to change: "there are three types of people in the world of change...those who make things happen, those who watch things happen, and then those who say, what the heck just happened?" Of course, it's not always that simple or obvious, but it is a good approximation of how people react to the reality of change. If not fully understood, and sometimes even when it is fully understood, change can be a bit frightening. Simply defined, change means to make or become different, to alter a thing from its current condition. Often you will find that people for the most part do not readily respond favorably to change or willingly accept it. Obama focused his newly appointed administration on the goal of obtaining a change that some have referred to as "the fundamental transformation of America."

There are many others who fit the UMA category. In fact, I cannot possibly name them all. I tried to focus primarily on some of the most popular voices in talk media news. Others who are not named in the title but are briefly mentioned in this book are **Mark Levin**, the so-called Great One, and **Neal Boortz**, the self-proclaimed "Talk Master."

I might also add that UMAs have been surfacing at one time or another in America's history. The main difference with today's is that we have much more powerful media resources like digital and cable television, satellite radio, the Internet, texting, e-mail, and more, which allow UMAs to reach the minds of multitudes of people very rapidly. Combined, these unchallenged and often unproven media resources can change the way millions of people think, respond, vote, live, and view one another and thus cause immeasurable and potentially dangerous change to our society.

8

So what's happening? As I began my research and writing, it was as if a veil were removed from my face. Yes, there was enlightenment, but accompanying my discoveries was a certain amount of fear. This fear was not just a feeling with no real substance; it originated out of the reality I found was destined to take place. I am still learning and have a strong desire to learn more. However, I now realize that all of the changes that are taking place in our day will most definitely affect our nation's current condition and our future forever. The America that we have known and may have loved is changing, and these changes were bound to happen. You will observe, just as I did, that these changes are due to public attitudes, perceptions, teachings, cultures, economics, and supporting geometrics. The persistent elements of power and greed have influenced the authorities of change. The changes are inevitable. The America that our parents grew up in and that many of us have known has passed away, and it will not be resurrected.

On January 8, 2011, America was devastated and shocked by a horrendous crime in Arizona. A mentally disturbed man, twenty-two years young, went on a shooting rampage, killing six people and wounding thirteen others. Among those pronounced dead were a prominent judge, John Roll; a wife of a former Marine, Dorothy Morris; a New Jersey native, Phyllis Schneck; a man who sacrificed his life to save his wife, Dorwan Stoddard; an outreach director, Gabe Zimmerman; and a nine-year-old girl who had been born September 11, Christina Taylor Green.

Among the wounded was a critically injured Democratic Representative, **Gabrielle Giffords**, also known as Gabby. Gabby suffered a head wound and was left in critical condition when a bullet fired at point-blank range entered the back of her skull and exited through the front of her head right above the left eyebrow.

In his anger, Pima County Sheriff Clarence Dupnik, a Democrat, expressed to the news media, "We need to do some soul searching. It's the vitriolic we hear day in and day out from people in the radio business and some in the TV

9

business. ...When you look at unbalanced people, how they respond to the vitriol that comes out of certain mouths about tearing down the government, the anger, the hatred, the bigotry that goes on in this country is getting to be outrageous."[15] There can be no doubt that this incident and the comments like these that were publicized in the media in the days that followed brought tremendous attention to the Ugly Mouths of America. As a result, the ugly mouths became furious. Rush Limbaugh, Sean Hannity, Glenn Beck, Mark Levin, and Neal Boortz all went on the defensive. Some even called for the removal of Sheriff Dupnik.

I visited Glenn Beck's website, (www.Glennbeck.com) and found on his blog the following post with regard to the shooting rampage: "However, the one thing no one seems to want to talk about is that after looking at the gunman and his ramblings, I don't see how a discussion about rhetoric applies at all. The truth is, unless there are a lot of new facts to come that we don't know about yet, this shooting say absolutely nothing about our political discourse. Nothing, in fact, it says absolutely nothing about our society as a whole. Zero."[16]

I have to admit that I had already started writing this before this horrifying crime took place. However, this shooting rampage made clear to me the necessity to make the public more aware of the effects and consequences of what we feed our eyes and ears and, through them, our minds. No, I am not blaming the Ugly Mouths of America for this crime. I do not believe unfounded blame should be placed on anyone. However, I must disagree with Mr. Beck and argue that this crime does, in fact, say something about our society. The very fact that this crime brings antigovernment, vitriolic public talk to our attention says something about our society. Since we are all interconnected in everyday living, there is always a positive or negative effect when engaging in conversation with a listening audience. When your conversation becomes a public discourse, a talk radio show, or a television program, there is a measure of responsibility you must take for how you affect your audience. If you are a popular host, your message moves your audience. That audience can easily become a very negative or a very positive force in society. As I mentioned at the start, the UMAs move millions of people, changing their ideas, their thinking, and their votes. Are these ugly mouths pundits of the news or just entertainers? They provide information, whether true or false, accurate or inaccurate, that is usually very strongly opinionated. Therefore, it's very important and even critical to our society that we take a closer look and examine the people we listen to.

The Ugly Mouths of America!

Chapter 1: A Look at the Rush

Rush Limbaugh currently hosts a three-hour radio program on the EIB (Excellence In Broadcasting) network. He has a website, www.rushlimbaugh.com. Limbaugh also became a best-selling author with two books, which are entitled *The Way Things Ought to Be* (1992) and *See, I Told You So* (1993). Rush acknowledges that he taped a recording of the first book and that it was transcribed and edited by *Wall Street Journal* writer John Fund. His second book was a collaboration with Joseph Farah of *WorldNetDaily*. In addition, he has written the forwards and introductions to several other books by other authors.

The one book with an introduction written by Limbaugh that really grabbed my attention was *Pimps, Whores and Welfare Brats: From Welfare Cheat to Conservative Messenger* (1997). The cover of this publication features a full color picture of an Afro-American woman. I can only imagine that the picture is of the author, Star Parker. Limbaugh's introduction includes a brief summary of the life of Star Parker and the difficult challenges she faced. Rush tells us how he met her in 1994 when she was on a television program that featured about twenty black Republicans. He goes on to say, "I believe the American dream is alive for any American willing to work hard and break through barriers blocking the path to prosperity." In the conclusion, he encourages every American to read Star Parker's inspirational story, "controversial as it may be in the black community."

To say the least, this book is very controversial. It received mixed reviews, especially from women in the black community. The title itself—*Pimps, Whores, and Welfare Brats*—came off as insulting to many. Star Parker's remarkable story of how she overcame many difficulties in her young life, including participating in a gang, abusing drugs, stealing, cutting school, burning a teacher's car, late-night partying, and having four abortions, is not the typical story of a person, black or white, who is raised on welfare. Although some, like Rush Limbaugh, marvel at her

12

accomplishments and her transformation to mainstream conservativeness, many take offense with her stereotypical views toward blacks. Often stereotypical depiction in movies and media news, it's the black man that steals, or belongs to a gang. It's the black women who is on welfare, uses drugs or have the abortion. Of course, by any standards, there are exceptions to every rule. However, there are many on welfare, both black and white, who have not involved themselves in crime, drugs and gangs. Apparently, Ms. Parker is not the typical welfare mother by any standards.

As I mentioned in the introduction, I was raised in Chicago in the 1960s and continued to live there until late 1997. I experienced life in the ghetto firsthand. Our family lived in the Englewood community, one of the most gang-infested areas on the south side of Chicago. My father worked full-time, putting in forty to forty-eight hours per week. My mother also worked full-time, mostly nights, so that our family was never on welfare. Even though we had only a modest income, our family was one of the wealthiest in the neighborhood. Approximately, four out of every five families of my inner circle of friends received some sort of government assistance at one time or another. The single-parent families and those with a part-time family-father who only visited on the weekends, they instilled a measure of integrity, honesty, and hard work in the majority of the kids in the hood. Both unseparated parents and single parents attended school board meetings and our basketball and baseball games, helped watch each other children, and pushed us to get good grades and an education so we could have overall better lives. This was a far cry from the stereotypical ghetto life depicted in Ms. Parker's publication.

There were the gangs, of course, and I knew many of the gangbangers, as they were called, through my older brother. However, even among the gangs you could find those desiring only to protect their own. Yes, the gangbangers of that time protected those who belonged to their neighborhood community. So neither our home of many years nor the homes of the friends we grew up with were ever broken into. Sometime individuals would get robbed at

13

gunpoint, but in most cases this took place outside of our community or when an opposing gang entered our turf.

When you visit the "about" section of Rush Limbaugh's website at www.RushLimbaugh.com, you are greeted with the following message: "The Rush Limbaugh show is the most listened to talk radio show in America, broadcast on over 600 radio stations nationwide. It's hosted by America Anchorman, Rush Limbaugh also known as: 'America Truth Detector; the Doctor of Democracy; the Most Dangerous Man in America; the All Knowing, All Sensing, All-Everything Maha Rushie; defender of motherhood, protector of fatherhood and an all-around good guy. There is a 'consensus' among the American people, who have made this the most listened to program, that it is also the most accurate, most right, and most correct. People who disagree with this are Rush Deniers."[1] Rush also says "that he is right 99.6% of the time." It amazes me that people can take seriously anything that comes out of this guy's mouth, but many millions do.

Rush Limbaugh claims to tell the news to the American public that the mainstream media refuses to report. But the question is whether his reports are accurate or factual. He talks about scientific matters as if he were a scientist or has confirmed his reports by the means of scientific research. For example, in his book *The Way Things Ought to Be*, Rush writes, "Mount Pinatubo in the Philippines spewed forth more than a thousand times the amount if ozone-depleting chemicals in one eruption than all the fluorocarbons manufactured by wicked, diabolical and insensitive corporations in history...Mankind can't possibly equal the output of even one eruption from Pinatubo, much less 4 billion years' worth of them, so how can we destroy the ozone layer?"[2] Of course, Rush believes that there is no such thing as global warming; according to him, "it's all one big scam."

Rush bashes Al Gore and talks down to anyone who calls in to his show. It does not matter what the credentials of the caller may be. If you disagree with Rush, you are an idiot or at least treated like one on the air. It is this type of

14

conversation that has become entertainment on his conservative talk show.

The facts of science prove that global warming is real. The question is only whether it is caused by man or nature. To answer Rush's question regarding volcanic eruptions like that of Mount Pinatubo, I refer to a report by the San Diego State University:

The halide acid HCl has been shown to be effective in destroying ozone; however, the latest studies show that most volcanic HCl is confined to the troposphere (below the stratosphere), where it is washed out by rain. Thus, it never has the opportunity to react with ozone. On the other hand, satellite data after the 1991 eruptions of Mt. Pinatubo (the Philippines) and Mt. Hudson (Chile) showed a 15-20% ozone loss at high latitudes and a greater than 50% loss over the Antarctic! Thus, it appears that volcanic eruptions can play a significant role in reducing ozone levels. However, it is an indirect role, which cannot be directly attributed to volcanic HCl. Eruption-generated particles, or aerosols, appear to provide surfaces upon which chemical reactions take place. The particles themselves do not contribute to ozone destruction, but they interact with chlorine- and bromine-bearing compounds from human-made CFCs. Fortunately, volcanic particles will settle out of the stratosphere in two or three years, so that the effects of volcanic eruptions on ozone depletion are short lived. Although volcanic aerosols provide a catalyst for ozone depletion, the real culprits in destroying ozone are human-generated CFCs. Scientists expect the ozone layer to recover due to restrictions on CFCs and other ozone-depleting chemicals by the United Nations Montreal Protocol on Substances that Deplete the Ozone Layer. However, future volcanic eruptions will cause fluctuations in the recovery process.[3]

Maybe Rush thinks this global warming scam is just an American scam. On the contrary, countries all over the world recognize climate change and its damaging effects on our planet's atmosphere. According to a *New York Times* science report, "Global warming has become perhaps the

15

most complicated issue facing world leaders. Warnings from the scientific community are becoming louder, as an increasing body of science points to rising dangers from the ongoing buildup of human-related greenhouse gases...The conflicts and controversies discussed are monotonously familiar: the differing obligations of industrialized and developing nations, the question of who will pay to help poor nations adapt, the urgency of protecting tropical forests and the need to rapidly develop and deploy clean energy technology."[4] So the debate should not be about whether global warming exists but about who will pay for the measures needed to correct the problem. Another facet of the debate is whether global warming is a natural occurrence or man-made. Historical data from ocean sediments and ice cores indicate cycles of warm interglacial periods for thousands of years. These cycles are separated by an ice age. We are currently in an interglacial period.[5] How much humans contributed to global warming, and if we can correct, or slow the process is the challenges we face. But, either way, global warming is real; it's not a debate, except, perhaps, in Rush Limbaugh's mind.

The Examiner featured an interesting article entitled "Rush Limbaugh, Global Warming and Susceptible Conservatives" by Jean Williams, a Seattle environmental policy examiner. In her article, she pinpoints how Rush runs his scam: "Rush Limbaugh claims global warming is a hoax and conservatives eat it up, while Limbaugh laughs all the way to the bank. The same is with his Fox News talk show cronies like Glenn Beck, Sean Hannity, Laura Ingraham...Creating fodder for their conservative audience is exactly what these commentators get paid for doing. So they go all out, including editing clips to show only what they want people to hear." [6]

Rush also entertains his daily audience by making fun of people with disabilities and, on other occasions, by making fun of people's nationalities. For example, the actor Michael J. Fox, who suffers from Parkinson's disease, had starred in a series of ads supporting candidates who favor stem cell research. In October 2006, Rush went on air and told his audience, "He is exaggerating the effects of the

16

disease…He's moving all around and shaking and it's purely an act. This is the only time I have ever seen Michael J. Fox portray any of the systems of the disease he had." Rush continued, "This is really shameless of Michael J. Fox. Either he didn't take his medicine or he's acting."[7] If you were to search Google or YouTube for videos of Rush making these foolish comments, you will see Rush moving around in his chair and talking and looking like an idiot. Here is the link for your observation: www.youtube.com/watch?v=xpFC9uziVhE Not only are his comments offensive, but they should also cause one to question the integrity and sanity of Mr. Limbaugh, who, by the way, is not a doctor. But, again, it is sad but true that facts tell the story, yet lies, often sells the story.

On another occasion, Rush Limbaugh mocked the president of China. On January 19, 2011, when commenting on air about Chinese President Hu Jintao's visit to the United States, Rush said to his audience, "[President Hu Jintao] was speaking and they weren't translating. They normally translate every couple of words. Hu Jintao was just going ching chong ching chong chon chon ching chee babababa…"[8] This insulting imitation of the Chinese language continued for about twenty seconds. As if that were not enough, later in the day on the same broadcast, he mocked the Chinese president again on the air. You would think that maybe the show producers or sponsors would caution him or even stop him from repeating such foolishness, but nope: apparently they just continued to go with the flow. Again, this is what sells.

Needless to say, the Chinese-American and the Asian-American communities were insulted by such childish behavior and gross disrespect. In fact, Representative David Wu, an Oregon Democrat and the first Chinese-American to serve in the US House of Representatives, said Limbaugh's comments indicated his "fundamental lack of character." He went on to say, "What begins as an ugly display quickly becomes striking for its pathetic childishness. Mr. Limbaugh proves once again his disinterest in civil and thoughtful discourse, and in doing so he ridicules one of the world's oldest languages, insults the Chinese-American and Asian-

17

American communities, and disrespects 1.3 billion people of China."[9]

Representative Judy Chu, a California Democrat and the first Chinese woman elected to the US House of Representatives, condemned Rush Limbaugh comments. "I was shocked and appalled by Rush Limbaugh's comments on his radio show yesterday. Calling the Chinese names and imitating the Chinese language was a childish and offensive tactic. It is one thing to disagree with a nation and criticize its policies, but it is another thing to demonize an entire people."[10]

But what can one really expect from the "American anchorman" who has absolutely no respect for the president of his own country? In fact, I would venture to say that I believe that Rush Limbaugh hates the current president of the United States of America more than any another US president in history. Based on his many public comments, he not only hates President Barack Obama but also despises Obama's wife, First Lady Michelle, and their two daughters, Sasha and Malia. Why would I go on record with such a bold statement? One can judge these things for him or herself by observing some of the many comments made publicly by Rush Limbaugh toward the first family.

Rush, for example, likes to ridicule Michelle Obama by calling her "Michelle My Belle," giving her a deep southern slang name. At times he has been even more demoralizing by referring to the first lady as "Moochelle" or "Michelle My Butt." Afterward, he often acts as if he misspoke. He has repeated this numerous times. He has gone on record as saying, "Some people were suggesting that my comments are below the belt. Well, take a look at some pictures. Given where she wears her belts, I mean, she wears them high up there around the bust line. Isn't just about everything about her below the belt, when you look at the fashion sense she has?"[11]

Rush Limbaugh also attacks the first lady's physical appearance and her anti-obesity campaigns. He called her a hypocrite after hearing of a report that she was served ribs at

18

a restaurant in Colorado. Rush went on a rampage, saying of Mrs. Obama, "The problem is, and I dare to say this, it doesn't look like Michelle Obama follows her own nutritionary, dietary advice. And then we hear that she's out eating ribs at 1,500 calories a serving with 141 calories of fat...I'm trying to say that our first lady does not project the image of women that you might see on the cover of the *Sports Illustrated* swimsuit issue or of a woman Alex Rodriguez might date every six months or what have you."[12]

With regard to President Obama's two daughters, Sasha and Malia, Mr. Limbaugh resorted to calling them fat. When mocking Obama's healthcare reform, which he likes to call "Obamacare," Rush said, "Since Obama just describe this wonderful system where his two daughters...two fat daughters, according to his wife...his two fat daughters came down with some sort of disease and had to rush them to the emergency room, why design a system that destroys the very best private health care that he says he's so thankful for?"[13] Anyone who sees a recent picture of Sasha and Malia could tell these young ladies are not fat.

When the TSA instituted a controversial screening procedure for checking people at the airports, Rush Limbaugh suggested that President Obama take his nine-year-old daughter to the airport and have the TSA groper go through the routine check on his daughter to prove it was safe.[14] Some consider the TSA screening to be a very invasive x-ray scan and /or an extensive pat down that may include the touching of private parts. For these reasons the screening procedure was highly criticized. First of all, the question of safety was not the main concern for the criticism; it was the invasion of privacy when searching or screening air travelers. Second, everyone did not receive this controversial screening procedure; primarily, it was adults. And just like the president and his family, Mr. Limbaugh flies on a private plane; he wants us to believe that he is like all of us, but like Obama, he does not have to go through this new screening process.

The verbal attacks on President Obama are too numerous to calculate. In the time that I have been listening

19

to Rush Limbaugh's talk radio show—nearly three years—I have never heard him refer to Barack Obama in a respectful manner as President Barack Obama. Instead he has referred to as "blithering idiot jackass," "Osama," a "halfrican American," an "angry black guy," "our first anti-American president," and "the greatest living example of a reverse racist." Rush has often played a song that refers to President Obama as "Barack the Magic Negro." It appears that Rush is keen on keeping racism alive, especially in the office of the White House.

This kind of talk promotes not only racism among his listeners but also hatred and division. Mr. Limbaugh is simply an entertainer who has the ability to make his reports and reasoning come off as factual and sound to the untrained and inexperienced listener. But the majority of mainstream news reporters and commentators and their audiences can detect the waves of foolishness in his discourse. The sad and surprising fact is that he continues to have an audience numbering in the millions. There are millions of minds that are wasting their time, losing their values, and being slowly manipulated by the controversial, racist, and disrespectful entertainment of Rush Limbaugh. All of this foolishness results in a profit to the tune of over $40 million per year going straight into Mr. Limbaugh's pocket. Even on the rare occasions when he makes a good, meaningful point or observation, it is accompanied with a spirit of disrespect and imbecilic criticism.

So, one may wonder, if all this is true about Rush, how could he have become so popular, powerful, and rich? The answer lies in the ruling of the Federal Communication Commission to abolish the Fairness Doctrine.

The Fairness Doctrine was a policy of the United States Federal Communications Commission (FCC) that was introduced in 1949. It was established to promote honesty, equitability, and balance in the presentation of controversial issues of importance to the public. Coverage of public issues was required to include a discussion of opposing views. In 1987, the FCC did away with the Fairness Doctrine, thus introducing the opportunity for one-

20

sided, very biased points of view to proliferate in public broadcasts. This allowed Rush Limbaugh and the UMAs to develop growing influence in the media.

Since 1987, this type of controversial, biased reporting has become more popular. There is no longer a need to broadcast an honest, fair, and balanced report; instead, increasing the size of an audience is the priority. It's a simple formula: the larger the audience, the greater the popularity; the greater the popularity, the greater the demand; the greater the demand, the more money in the pockets of networks, producers, and entertainers. The sad, negative side to this type of reporting is that the audience becomes more confused, ignorant, and misled, and these characteristics are often accompanied by the development of disgruntled attitudes.

Rush Limbaugh was not always a popular voice in conservative radio. If we look back on Rush's life, we will find that he was your typical well-to-do young man who never finished college. He was never really poor, as he wants us to believe, but rather, his grandfather and father were lawyers. His brother, David Limbaugh, is also a lawyer and an author. His uncle, Stephen N. Limbaugh Sr., was appointed by President Ronald Regan as a federal judge in the district of Missouri. So, he comes from a well-to-do family; it was only Rush who had been doing basically nothing and dropped out of college.

In 1972, after dropping out of college, he became a Top 40 music disc jockey in Pennsylvania. He broadcast under the name "Jeff Christie." In 1973 he moved to a Pittsburg station, and in 1974 he was fired when the station was sold to Taft Broadcasting. It was reportedly said of Mr. Limbaugh "that he would never make it as on-air talent and he should consider going into sales."[15]

Even though Rush has been very successful on the air, this advice still remains true to some extent. He has no real on-air radio talent. He stutters often when he is excited, mispronounces words, and really does not have a radio personality that exudes any professionalism. But he is

21

definitely a salesman. He sells false information, criticism, and foolishness as featured news in order to keep his audience entertained and misled.

In 1979, after working at several different radio stations, Rush left radio altogether. He became a director of promotions with the Kansas City Royals baseball team. According to Rush, he was fired from them, too.

In 1984, Rush returned to radio as a talk show host in Sacramento, California. And in 1987, when the Fairness Doctrine was abolished under Ronald Regan, "Rush Limbaugh was," according to *Wall Street Journal* editor Daniel Henninger, "the first man to proclaim himself liberated from the East Germany of liberal media domination."[16] And the foolishness began.

Rush has been married four times. In 1977, he married Roxy Maxine McNeely. They got divorced on the grounds of "incompatibility" in 1980. Three years later, he married Michelle Sixta. Maybe this is when he develop all the offensive names he now has for Michelle Obama. In 1990, they got divorced. Four years later, he married Marta Fitzgerald; he divorced her in 2004. Finally, in June 2010, he married his fourth wife, Kathryn Rogers. At the time of this writing, she is still his wife (as far as I am able to tell).

Rush Limbaugh has also had his share of drug addictions and arrests. In October 2003, the Palm Beach state attorney began to conduct a three-year investigation into Mr. Limbaugh after he publicly admitted his addiction to pain medicine and entrance into a rehab program. In October 2003, Rush said on his radio program, "I need to tell you today that part of what you have heard and read is correct. I am addicted to prescription pain medicine."[17] The investigation led to the arrest and booking of Limbaugh in April 2006 in Palm Beach County. He was charged with fraud to conceal information to obtain prescriptions. Basically, he was said to be "doctor shopping," or illegally deceiving multiple doctors to receive overlapping prescriptions.[18]

22

Acting like a crooked politician, Rush was able to get the charges dropped without a guilty plea after he made a deal to continue his rehabilitation treatments of eighteen months with his doctor of two years. His rehab program caused him to miss about five weeks from his radio program. According to an agreement with the Palm Beach County state's attorney's office, Limbaugh also had to pay $30,000 to defray the costs of the investigation, as well as $30 a month for his supervision.[19]

Prior to his arrest, Mr. Limbaugh was a very outspoken critic of those who use drugs illegally. In October 1995, on his short-lived television program, he made the following comments:

There is nothing good about drug use. We know it. It destroys individuals. It destroys families. Drug use destroys societies. Drug use, some might say, is destroying this country. And we have laws against selling drugs, pushing drugs, using drugs, importing drugs. And the laws are good because we know what happens to people in societies and neighborhoods which become consumed by them. And so if people are violating the law by doing drugs, they ought to be accused and they ought to be convicted and they ought to be sent up.

What this says to me is that too many whites are getting away with drug use. Too many whites are getting away with drug sales. Too many whites are getting away with trafficking the stuff. The answer to this disparity is not to start letting people out of jail because we're not putting others in jail that are breaking the law. The answer is to go out and find the ones who are getting away with it, convict them, and send them up the river, too.

…We are becoming too tolerant as a society, folks, especially of crime, in too many parts of the country…This country certainly appears to be tolerant, forgive and forget. I mean, you know as well as I do, you go out and commit the worst murder in the world and you just say you're sorry, people go, "Oh, OK. A little contribution."…People say, "I

23

feel better. He said he's sorry for it." We're becoming too tolerant, folks."[20]

According to Rush's own words, he should have been in jail.

Earlier in the same month that he admitted to his drug addiction, Mr. Limbaugh was relieved from ESPN after making racial comments regarding three-time Pro Bowler, runner-up for the most valuable player award, and former Philadelphia Eagles quarterback Jonathan McNabb. Rush said in his commentary regarding McNabb, "I don't think that he's been that good from the get-go. I think what we've had here is a little social concern in the NFL. This media has been very desirous that a black quarterback do well. There is little hope invested in McNabb, and he got a lot of credit for the performance of his team that he didn't deserve. The defense carried this team."[21] The following week ESPN accepted Rush Limbaugh's resignation.

One might think his comments regarding Jonathan McNabb were not really racially motivated or that maybe Rush was only expressing his opinion. But anyone who follows football, either on a professional or college level, knows that the quarterback is always primarily credited with the success or failure of his team. The reason is that the team cannot win a single game if they cannot score. It is the quarterback's responsibility to move the ball gradually down the field, put the team in the position to score, score, keep his defensive team off the field so they can have regular and much-needed rest, and tire out the opposing team's defense and keep them guessing. The quarterback has always been the captain or general in charge and the most important position on any football team.

It is worthwhile to consider something that can be found in the holy scriptures of the Bible to understand the meaning of the ugly mouth of Rush Limbaugh and his undermining attitude. Whether one considers him or herself a Christian or not, one can't truly argue with this fact that is found in Mathew 15:18, which reads, "However, the things proceeding out of the mouth comes out of the heart, and those things defile a man." In fact, this scripture can be applied to anyone who has the ability to express him or herself in words. The words that come out of our mouths make up our viewpoints, our visions, our feelings, our realities, and our paradigms.

So what can we conclude from Rush Limbaugh's words? We observe a man who is a renowned figure in television and talk radio. He expresses controversial viewpoints that are inaccurate, antigovernmental, disrespectful, demeaning, racial, and hypocritical. His popularity has grown to an audience of fifteen to twenty million listeners each week. He has the unique ability to sound like the average guy you may meet on the street when in reality he is a multimillionaire who makes money by selling propaganda that stirs controversy. Mr. Limbaugh's popularity becomes an influential resource to the tune of big businesses advertising commercial products and promotions, as well as political opportunities, were politicians attempt to gain his support and the votes of his audience.

I am not alone in this opinion of Mr. Limbaugh. The following words were expressed in an article in *The Seattle Times*, winner of eight Pulitzer Prizes, after Rush Limbaugh said "he hoped President Obama fails." The article's headline was "Rush Limbaugh's a disloyal clown when he says he hopes Obama fails," and the following makes up part of its content:

It is, of course, a calculated outrage.

Meaning, it was spewed by a clown in the media circus to kick a familiar sequence into motion: angry denunciation by bloggers, pundits and supporters of President Obama (the "he" whose failure is hoped), followed by Rush Limbaugh refusing to retract a word, a courageous truth teller who will not be moved. And, trailing behind, like the folks with brooms trail the elephants in the circus parade, Limbaugh's devotees, complaining that their hero has been misquoted, misunderstood, or otherwise mistreated. "What Rush meant was…yadda yadda yadda."…

Do you ever say that about your president if you are an American who loves your country? Would you say it about George W. Bush, who was disastrous, about Bill Clinton, who was slimy, about Jimmy Carter, who was inept, about Richard Nixon, who was crooked? You may think he's going to fail, yes. You may warn he's going to fail, yes.

But do you ever "hope" he fails? Knowing his failure is the country's failure? Isn't that, well…disloyal?

The irony is that Limbaugh and the other clowns would have you believe they are bedrock defenders of this country, that they love it more than the rest of us, more than anything.

That's a lie. Limbaugh just told us so, emphatically.

It's not the country they love. It's the attention. The ideology, their perversion of conservatism, is but a means toward that end.[22]

The conclusion I draw is that Rush Limbaugh is a broadcast entertainer and not an expert news commentator by any means. He is a salesman and a storyteller. As a storyteller, he often stutters in excitement, sometimes mumbling his words; he lacks professionalism, and he does not necessarily tell us the truth but instead sells his side of the story, which is often fabricated.

Just like any other businessman, politician, gang leader, or drug dealer, Rush has a group of comrades or cronies, followers who have joined themselves to the growing prosperity and popularity of facetious media controversies that encourage very dangerous attitudes.

The Ugly Mouths of America!

Chapter 2: The Hannitization of America

In 2004, Sean Hannity referred to his program as "the Hannitizing of America." So I decided to take a look at the man who claims to be Hannitizing our country. If you visit his website, www.hannity.com, you will not, just as with Rush Limbaugh, observe any signs of modesty or humility, traits, I might add, that most great men possess. In the "about" section of his website, it says, "Sean Hannity is a multimedia superstar, spending four hours a day, every day reaching out to millions of Americans on radio, television, and internet."[1]. It goes on to tell us that the Sean Hannity Show on the radio has roughly 13.5 million loyal listeners a week, making him the second most listened to talk show host in America, behind Rush Limbaugh.

Sean Hannity was born December 30, 1961. His parents, Hugh J. and Lillian F. Hannity, were emigrates from Ireland. He grew up in Franklin Square, New York, and attended school at Sacred Heart Seminary in Hempstead; his high school was St. Pius X Preparatory Seminary in Uniondale, New York. So Hannity has a Catholic educational background. Like Rush, Hannity dropped out of college; he briefly attended New York University and Adelphi University

Sean is a very successful author of several best-selling books: *Let Freedom Ring: Winning the War of Liberty over Liberalism, Deliver Us from Evil: Defeating Terrorism, Despotism, and Liberalism,* and in 2010, *Conservative Victory: Defeating Obama's Radical Agenda.* It was the promotion of his first book that launched the "Hannitization of America" tour in 2002. This tour proved to be very successful and involved Sean traveling the United States, publishing his views and promoting his book.

The phrase "let freedom ring" may sound familiar to you, because these words were repeated in Dr. Martin Luther King's famous "I Have a Dream" discourse, given in Washington, DC, on August 28, 1963. Dr. King spoke about the need to liberate Black America from the oppression of second-class citizenship and to end the mistreatment and

27

condescension blacks suffered by whites due to the color of their skin and the appearance of their faces. Dr. King said, in part, "And when this happens, when we allow freedom ring, when we let it ring from every village and every hamlet, from every state and every city, we will be able to speed up that day when all of God's children, black men and white men, Jews and Gentiles, Protestants and Catholics, will be able to join hands and sing the words of the old Negro spiritual, 'Free at last! Free at last! Thank God Almighty, we are free at last!'"[2]

So what exactly is the "Hannitization of America"? Does Hannity's use of the expression "let freedom ring" suggest that it is part of the dream expressed by Dr. Martin Luther King? Is it part of the dream that one day all of God's children will be free? Hardly. When Sean Hannity cohosted a Fox Radio program with liberal Alan Colmes, Hannity would often end the program with the phrase "let freedom ring." This sounded very patriotic and emotional and was reminiscent to the days of Dr. King and the civil rights movement. However, the "Hannitization of America" has a different objective than these did. Explaining his mission in December 2007, *CBS Morning Program* put it simply: "Conservatives equals good. Liberal is bad."[3]

There is no doubt that Hannity has extreme right-wing conservative views. But his viewpoint that all liberalism is bad or evil, as expressed in his book *Deliver Us from Evil: Defeating Terrorism, Despotism and Liberalism*, makes me wonder whether he's being at all accurate or scrupulous. In fact, liberalism led to the freedom rights movement of the 1950s and early 1960s. "Liberal," simply defined, means to be tolerant and to respect individual freedom, according to the *Oxford English Dictionary and Thesaurus*. It was these very grass roots movements and marches for freedom against the conservative, restrictive America of that time that help set the standards for the country we live in today.

Sean Hannity builds his popularity and wealth on the blocks of patriotism. Everyone who agrees with him is said to be "a great American." Those who disagree with him are labeled idiots, stupid, lunatics, and ignorant of the facts. As

28

Sean related he has mastered the art of arguing. Using this "gift", his ability to argue, Sean Hannity makes his viewpoints sound natural and sometimes reasonable to his listeners. For example, he fights for the rich or, as he often says, the "high achievers," as if he were not one of the super-rich himself. Hannity makes out like he is protecting the poor and middle class by empowering the rich. Please do not misunderstand my point here: there is nothing wrong with working hard, making an honest and moral living, and reaping the rewards of your labor and ingenuity. This is the way it should be. But on the other side of the coin, there are organizations and individuals—and they are many—who have wrongfully taken tremendous advantage of the political, financial, commercial, and religious systems of our society to accumulate their wealth. A well-known author and philanthropist, Napoleon Hill, who wrote *Think and Grow Rich* and promoted *The Science of Personal Achievement*, was once asked, "What is success?" His answer was short but very distinctive and to the point: "That success is the ability to get anything you want out of life *without violating the rights of other people*." (emphasis mine)

We do need people to be successful, and these individuals and organizations should obtain an increase in wealth as a result of their accomplishments. However, violating the rights of other people to do so indicates a lack of morals and human principles, the things that have their basis rooted in the Bible. Let's be perfectly clear: I'm not talking about all of the rich. But I am talking about many of them. They are politicians, clergies, entertainers, commentators, big business corporations, lobbyists, stockbrokers, and others who have learned to take advantage of a system, find loopholes, and in the rules of engagement exploit them. They align themselves with like individuals and thus take advantage of the ignorant or unknowing general public.

Mr. Hannity makes millions of dollars each year by sounding off as a so-called great American. He's paid to give very strong, right-wing, opinionated views of politics and current news. He comes across as one of us, a hardworking American who is struggling to survive in this system,

29

concerned about his children and his grandchildren. He is the major promoter of a charity organization called Freedom Alliance, founded by his close friend and business associate Col. Oliver North in 1999.

Freedom Alliance puts on freedom concerts all across America. According to Freedom Alliance these concerts are "a dynamic, patriotic celebration of America and her heroes hosted by radio and television personality Sean Hannity ..."[4] Some of his fans and devoted listeners have expressed a strong desire for Mr. Hannity to become a politician and run for office. However, Hannity has said that he will never become a politician. He loves the job he currently has as well as being a voice for the people. This all sounds good and suggests he acts as a true "great American" would on the surface, but let's take an inside look at Mr. Hannity and his charitable organization. While doing so, let's also keep in mind that true success does not violate the rights or morally take advantage of other people.

If you were to visit www.FreedomAlliance.org, you would find the following mission statement in their "about us" section: "The Mission of Freedom Alliance is to advance the American heritage of freedom by honoring and encouraging military service, defending the sovereignty of the United States and promoting a strong national defense. Freedom Alliance is an educational and charitable organization which sponsors numerous program activities aimed at supporting and honoring our service members and their families."[5]

Then it breaks down the educational and charitable initiatives being taken by the group with four main programs:

The **Support Our Troops** program honors members of our Armed Forces who secure the liberty with which God has blessed us. To recognize their service, we host events to express our thanks and appreciation to our military; provide financial and other help to our troops in a time of need; and honor and assist their families.

The **Military Leadership Academy (MLA)** inspires, educates and motivates young Americans to become

30

positive, productive citizens and leaders in their communities and among their peers. The program teaches students leadership principles based on Freedom Alliance's Core Values of Selfless Service, Courage, Dependability, Integrity, Responsibility, Respect and Teamwork.

Our **Public Policy initiative** educates the American people about the need to protect our national sovereignty and national defense. We host educational seminars and conferences to inform the public about these issues of national importance.

Freedom Alliance's **Scholarship Fund** provides college scholarships to the sons and daughters of American heroes—the dependents of U.S. military personnel who have been killed or permanently disabled in an operational mission or training accident. We do this for two reasons: first, to help deserving students with the rising cost of college education; and second, to remind those students that their parents' sacrifices will never be forgotten by a grateful nation.[6]

Feigning to build on the blocks of patriotism, Sean Hannity and Oliver North's so-called charitable organization has become a successful moneymaking-machine with multimillion dollar profits. Let's examine the facts regarding Freedom Alliance to see where the money and revenue really goes.

Debbie Schlussel, a well-known conservative political commentator, radio talk show host, columnist, and attorney, blew the whistle and exposed Hannity's Freedom Alliance. In March 2010, she published an article on her website entitled "Sean Hannity's Freedom Concert Scam." Here are her findings:

Almost None of Charity $ Went to Injured Troops, Kids of Fallen Troops; G5 for Vannity?

In fact, less than 20%—and in two recent years, less than 7% and 4%, respectively—of the money raised by Freedom Alliance went to these causes, while millions of dollars went

31

to expenses, including consultants and apparently to ferry the Hannity posse of family and friends in high style. And, despite Hannity's statements to the contrary on his nationally syndicated radio show, few of the children of fallen soldiers got more than $1,000–$2,000, with apparently none getting more than $6,000, while Freedom Alliance appears to have spent tens of thousands of dollars for private planes. Moreover, despite written assurances to donors that all money raised would go directly to scholarships for kids of the fallen heroes and not to expenses, has begun charging expenses of nearly $500,000 to give out just over $800,000 in scholarships.[7]

These were not just accusations. Ms. Schlussel provided the proof by hyperlinking to Freedom Alliance's tax reports. According to its 2006 tax return, Freedom Alliance had revenues of $10,822,785 but only $397,900 was given as scholarships to the children of fallen troops or as aid to severely injured soldiers.

If you do the math, less than four percent—actually 3.68%—of the revenue earned went to the cause of the charity. To put that into perspective, it's as if you were to give me a dollar to give to someone who's in need and I were to keep ninety-six cents of that dollar and give the needy person a measly four cents. I rightfully suggest that, in that situation, you would conclude that I was being misleading and perhaps call me a thief. The same should be the case for Sean Hannity's Freedom Alliance.

You may wonder where all the money went and whether anything has changed since this information has been made public. Let's examine Freedom Alliance's public tax reports from 2006 and beyond. According to the 2006 tax returns, 62 percent of its earned revenue ($6,710,126) went to expenses. That includes $979, 485 that went to so-called consultants and advisors. That is more than double the amount of money that went to the children of fallen troops. As Ms. Schlussel reports, "And finally, that year, Freedom Alliance spent $1,730,816 on postage and shipping and $1,414,215 on printing, for a total of $3,145,031, nearly half

32

the revenue the charity spent that year and about eight times what the injured troops and the children of fallen ones received."[8]

The following describes some examples of Freedom Alliance's "generous" giving acts. In 2006, Freedom Alliance gave only $1,000 to a soldier from Bay City, Michigan, whose face, the charity said, "was blown up" and who had "lost vision in one eye." Freedom Alliance gave $200 to a soldier from Romulus, Michigan, a predominantly black area; this soldier had lost both legs and his left arm in a roadside bomb incident in Iraq.[9] That means Freedom Alliance gave about sixty-seven dollars per limb. I agree with Debbie Schlussel: "that's sickening!"

In a case in 2006, another soldier from Alexandria, Virginia, received a whopping $200 from Freedom Alliance. This soldier had been wounded in an explosion in Iraq and suffered severe wounds to the upper body and face and loss of the right arm.[10]

If you see this the way I do, Mr. Hannity no longer appears to be a "great American" but rather a great American con artist! He rakes in hundreds of thousands of dollars each year to spend on fancy limousines, lucrative vacations, and high-end entertainment, all thanks to Freedom Alliance.

The scam continued in 2007. Freedom Alliance's tax report for 2008 showed that the charity scam took in revenues of $12,459,317 and out of that bundle, only 7 percent ($895,347) went to severely wounded soldiers and the scholarship fund for children of fallen soldiers.[11]

As reported by Debbie Schlussel and confirmed by Freedom Alliance's 2007 tax forms, one soldier who was wounded in Iraq on June 18, 2007, by an IED explosion took a shrapnel to the face, cutting off part of the nose. Other shrapnel cut the soldier's cheeks and sliced open his throat. Freedom Alliance gave that soldier $500.[12]

33

A soldier from Brady, Texas, was also hit by an IED blast in 2007. This soldier reportedly sustained disfigurement, blindness, and superficial burns on the face, suffered hearing loss in the right ear, and "TBI, peppered shrapnel to the face and right upper extremity." Freedom Alliance gave that soldier $500.[13]

In 2008, Freedom Alliance reported total revenue as $8,781,431. According to its tax forms for that year, it gave just 12 percent ($1,060,275.57) to seriously wounded soldiers and to the scholarships for children of the fallen troops. While 12 percent may sound better than the previous year's allotment, it is important to note here that a charity is only considered reputable and respectful if no more than 25 percent of its revenue goes toward expenses and no less than 75 percent of its revenue goes to the intended charity recipients. I agree with Ms. Schlussel: "Given that, Freedom Alliance's balance sheets are embarrassing in their shamelessness."[14]

In April 2008, a soldier from Laurel, MD, lost both legs, his arm below the elbow, and hearing in both ears due to an IED blast. Freedom Alliance gave that soldier the ridiculously low amount of just $1000.[15]

A soldier from Houston, Texas, suffered 30 percent facial burns and became a bilateral amputee due to an IED blast in May 2008. Freedom Alliance gave this soldier a pathetic $165.[16]

These are not just a few isolated cases; the public tax record of Sean Hannity's freedom concerts used to promote Freedom Alliance is disgusting but transparent. In fact, I believe I could write an entire book on the subject of Freedom Alliance. This charity prospers from misleading statements made by Hannity as well as big advertisement centered on the theme of patriotism. Most people are willing to give support to the injured troops who have served our country and to the children of our fallen soldiers. But we want our money to actually go to these people, not into Hannity's gigantic pockets of greed.

When Sean Hannity travels to and from freedom concerts, he takes a private plane (usually a Gulfstream 5). Upon landing, he and his entourage are driven to the events in a fleet of limousines, which further strokes Sean's ego. He stays in suites at very expensive hotels and eats at the very best restaurants. These are just some of the things counted as expenses for Freedom Alliance's charitable events. I'm also quite sure that Mr. Hannity is paid well for his superstar appearances.

Debbie Schlussel blew the lid off of Freedom Alliance, which led others to investigate the charity even further. In March 2010, an article was released that included the following quotation from a Washington organization called Citizens for Responsibility and Ethics in Washington (CREW):

Today, Citizens for Responsibility and Ethics in Washington (CREW) filed complaints with the Federal Trade Commission (FTC) and the Internal Revenue Service (IRS) against Sean Hannity, his Freedom Concerts, the Freedom Alliance and Lt. Col. Oliver North. Copies of the complaints were also sent to the attorney generals of the states in which concerts are scheduled to be held this summer.

CREW's FTC complaint alleges Hannity and Freedom Concerts have engaged in illegal and deceptive marketing practices by suggesting that all money generated by ticket sales for the Freedom Concerts he sponsors each summer goes to scholarships for children of killed and wounded service members. In fact, the concerts are staged by Premiere Marketing, which is headed by Duane Ward—also the head of Premiere Speakers Bureau, which exclusively represents Mr. Hannity and Lt. Col. North. After staging the concerts, Premiere donates an unknown portion of the concert proceeds to the Freedom Alliance.

Hannity has promoted the concerts on his show, making statements such as, "Every penny, 100 percent of the donations are applied to the Freedom Alliance scholarship fund." Similarly, promoting the concert on Hannity's program,

35

Lt. Col. North has said, "There's no overhead. There's no expenses taken out. Every penny that's donated or that's raised through things like the Freedom Concerts goes to the scholarship fund." In addition, Hannity has pledged that all the proceeds of his new book, *Conservative Victory*, will go to Freedom Alliance.

CREW's IRS complaint against Freedom Alliance asks the IRS to consider revoking its charitable tax status because the organization has engaged in prohibited political activities. When Freedom Alliance first formed in 1999, the IRS conditioned its charitable tax status on the organization removing politically partisan materials from its website and warned it not to intervene in political campaigns. Despite those warnings, Freedom Alliance's website includes links to Lt. Col. North's columns, which are largely political, rents its mailing list to a communications firm that works for organizations that "seek to reach Republicans and conservatives across the United States," and hosts an annual "Freedom Cruise" with Republican politicians such as former House Speaker Newt Gingrich and Republican National Committee Chairman Michael Steele. In addition, Freedom Alliance appears to have a relationship with Team America, a PAC formed by Rep. Tom Tancredo (R-CO), dedicated to anti-immigration efforts and supporting conservative candidates.[17]

This shows just how far Hannity is from being a great American, a responsible citizen, or a Christian. In fact, *The First Church of Free Speech* by Jason Peppers, filed on August 12, 2007, under "News, Politics and Religion," made this statement: "Sean Insanity has been travelling the country on his so-called 'freedom concert' tour (were they once called French concerts?). These shows are promoted as benefit concerts to raise money to send the children of servicemen who died in Iraq to college. As it turns out, they are nothing but a scam to fleece the cud-chewers who still think the war is a wonderful thing."[18]

A writer at *Daily Kos* calling himself "Dave From Queens" did a little snooping around. Guess what he found?

KFMB   Radio   wrote:
WHERE: COORS AMPHITHEATRE IN CHULA VISTA, CA.
2050 Entertainment Circle, Chula Vista, CA 91911
WHEN: Thursday – July 26, 2007 7:30 PM (Doors open at
5:30   PM)
TICKETS: Prices: **$38.00 - $78.00** PURCHASE TICKETS
The following fees are included in the above ticket prices:
$4.75 facility fee, $4.25 parking fee, and a **$4.00 donation
to the Freedom Alliance.**[18] (emphasis mine)

So, does Sean Hannity intend to Hannitize America by scamming its citizens? As I listened to Mr. Hannity and continued in my research, I realized that he and Rush Limbaugh have quite a few things in common. This also reminds me of an old saying my mother often repeated: "Birds of a feather flock together," or as the Bible reads, "Likewise, every good tree produces fine fruit, but every rotten tree produces worthless fruit...Really, then, by their fruits you will recognize those [men]." (Matthew 7:17-20).

Unlike Rush Limbaugh, Mr. Hannity is far more than just an entertainer. He seems to actually have deeply embedded concerns about what is happening within our country and for the future of America. Often during his broadcast, he will speak about his children, his family, or friends, expressing how they may be affected by the news of the day. In addition, he regularly has visiting politicians, authors, and commentators on his program. However, it has been noted that he claims he will never run for political office or get in the mix of making governing decisions. Rather, he has chosen to be chauffeured in limos and build a financial empire upon the patriotic emotions of others.

In the media Sean Hannity is, like Rush Limbaugh, known for stretching the truth and sometimes just plain fabricating the news. For example, in November 2009, Sean Hannity and his sponsor, Americans for Prosperity, held an anti–health care rally in Washington, DC. Sean reported that

37

there was a turnout of over twenty thousand people. His television program showed a video of a great crowd of people who had gathered for the event. In fact, however, to make the event appear to have this large crowd, Fox News used video from a Glenn Beck rally. You can view this hysterical piece of fantasy news at www.newscorpse.com/ncWP/?p=1450.

Afterward, the following was posted on the *News Corpse* website under the headline "Sean Hannity's Lies Exposed by Jon Stewart":

The propagandists at Fox are well aware that the nation overwhelmingly supports heath care reform, so they resort to dishonesty in pursuit of their unpopular agenda. If they can't get enough Tea Baggers to show up, Fox will just falsify the video record to make whatever point serves their venal interests. It is the same disrespect for the truth that compels Hannity to assert, without any evidence, that 20,000+ people turned out to the protest, although neutral sources say it was no more than 10,000. Hannity's guest, Rep. Michele Bachmann (R-MN), put the crowd estimate as high as 45,000. She also said that the event was the result of spontaneous word of mouth. What she left out was that Fox News promoted the affair repeatedly and anti–health care lobbyists like Americans for Prosperity funded the organizing efforts, including some forty buses to deliver the AstroTurfers to the Capital.

What's truly depressing about all of this (besides Hannity keeping his job) is that the rest of the media has failed to report any of it. When Dan Rather aired a true story that was marred by a few poorly vetted documents, it became a media frenzy that eventually cost Rather his job. But when Hannity blatantly manufactures a false story, the media shrugs its shoulders and turns away…[19]

After being exposed by Jon Stewart, Mr. Hannity admitted that they "screwed up" by using the "incorrect video." He called it "an inadvertent mistake." Mr. Hannity did not specifically address how the mistake came to be made, but
38

he did say, somewhat ruefully, "It pains me to say: Jon Stewart was right."[20]

Here is a second example of Sean Hannity's many fabrications. In August 2011, Sean Hannity reported that when President Obama took office, "he inherited unemployment at 5.6 percent."[21] According to the US Department of Labor, however, unemployment at that time was actually around 7.6 percent. The reason for this high unemployment rate was expressed in these words by *US News Money*:

What in the world is going on? The job market is simply continuing to deteriorate. Companies are cutting costs to make up for plummeting demand and a lack of available credit and investment. As the recession has deepened, job losses have become increasingly broad—now touching nearly all sectors of the economy. Manufacturing is bleeding jobs—the sector lost 207,000 jobs in January, the biggest loss since October 1982, according to the Labor Department. Construction lost 111,000, bringing the total jobs lost in construction to 1 million since January of 2007. The retail, transportation, and financial sectors all continued to cut payrolls. One bright spot: The health care industry and private education actually added jobs during the month.[22]

In April 2011, Sean Hannity bluntly blamed President Obama for the mortgage crisis. It's a known fact that the mortgage crisis and the so-called real estate bubble disaster happened in 2006, two years before President Obama was elected. It appears that, to Hannity, whatever happens in this country, both during and before, and perhaps even after Obama's presidency is Obama's fault. He finds a way to blame the president for everything negative and even to turn a positive outcome into a negative one.

I am by no means saying that some of the current crises our country is experiencing are not the direct result of Obama's administrative policies; however, as a reporter or so-called commentator, Mr. Hannity needs to make sure of the accuracy of his statements and tell an unbiased story to

39

the listening public. That can also be said of all the UMAs' profoundly opinionated reporting style. If they do choose to include their opinion in their reports, why do they need to fabricate the story? Great Americans would not and do not conduct themselves in this way.

Hannity often interviews others, both those who agree with his point of view and those who have an opposing one. On the surface this sounds all good and fair, but in reality, he gives more time and more favorable coverage to the ones who agree with him and often interrupts, makes rude remarks, and asks meaningless questions to the guests who have views opposed to his. These latter interviews usually end up as what sounds like a confusing, confrontational argument, which prevents the opposing view from being clearly heard and understood. I guess this is what is meant by "Hannitizing America."

In March 2008, Malik Zulu Shabazz of the New Black Panther Party appeared as a guest on *Hannity & Colmes* to discuss Obama's alleged association with Reverend Wright and Shabazz's organizational endorsement of Barack Obama, which had been rejected. During that appearance, Sean Hannity asked Mr. Shabazz whether Barack Obama shouldn't be judged for his past affiliations with Reverend Wright, to which Shabazz countered by asking Sean Hannity, "Should you be judged by your past association with Hal Turner, a neo-Nazi?"[23] This interchange of words followed:

Hannity: "What I don't think you're understanding here, Malik, is that when you hear the minister of him for twenty years, when you hear the associations with Louis Farrakhan, one of the biggest racists and anti-Semites in the country, what you're not understanding is, America hears extremism at its worst."

Shabazz: "Let me ask you this. Are you to be judged by your promotion and association with Hal Turner?"

40

Hannity: "I don't know anybody named—this is nonsense. I don't..." Then Hannity changed his tune from denying he did not know Hal Turner, to explaining their past relationship. "Sir, sir...That was a man that was banned from my radio show ten years ago, that ran a Senate campaign in New Jersey."

(Shabazz refused to stop talking, so Hannity speaks over him)

Hannity: "I'm not running for president."

Shabazz: "A neo-Nazi, you backed his career."[24]

Hal Turner, born Charles Harold Turner on March 15, 1962, is a white supremacist, neo-Nazi, ex–talk radio host, and blogger from North Bergen, New Jersey. According to *The Hartford Courant*, he was arrested for inciting violence in June 2009. Turner allegedly incited Catholics to "take up arms," singling out two Connecticut lawmakers and a state ethics official as targets of this violence. Mr. Turner is no stranger to controversy and has issued threats to public figures in the past. In August 2010, he was convicted for making threats against three federal judges with the Seventh US Circuit Court of Appeals. Prior to Turner's arrest, his radio program, *The Hal Turner Show*, was webcast from his home once a week.

In light of Sean Hannity's comments, Turner subsequently posted the following response on his website: "I was quite disappointed when Sean Hannity at first tried to say he didn't know me. In fact, Sean does know me and we were quite friendly a few years ago."[25]

It is a fact that Hal Turner at one time frequently called Sean Hannity's radio show and was given airtime. With regard to the closeness of their relationship, there are conflicting stories. But according to Newsvine.com, in March 2008, Hal Turner offered to release Sean Hannity's tapes of their conversations both on and off the air for $100,000 and

41

to sell the tapes outright for $250,000. He reportedly wanted the money by April 15, 2008. The following is a translated excerpt of the offer made by Hal Turner's website:

Since more than 100,000 of you read the story on Huffington Post about me being friendly with Hannity years ago, I made an offer on my radio show tonight:

I will release to the public, all the tape recordings I have between me and Sean Hannity both on and off the air IF, by April 15, 2008, those 100,000 readers of Huffington Post send me one dollar (or more) each until such time as I receive One-Hundred-Thousand Dollars ($100,000.) AND the deadline for the money arriving is April 15. If I receive the $100K by April 15, I will release via tape, CD and download from this site, all the "dicey" conversations we had. If I do not receive at least $100,000, by April 15, I will not release the tapes.

I will not speculate or make any representations about what is on those tapes, but suffice it to say I think there is material on them that you will find VERY useful!

In addition to the offer above, I am willing to SELL the tapes, complete ownership of their content and all broadcast rights forever to anyone willing to buy them for two hundred fifty thousand dollars ($250,000).

If there is a conflict between the $100,000 coming and the $250,000, I agree to REFUND the $100K less postage to whoever donates.

I am willing to post a LIST OF ALL DONATIONS citing only the amount, form of payment and postmark so all of you can see each day how much comes in. Complete transparency!

That's the offer. Those of you who hate Sean Hannity have a chance to pony-up. Those of you who want to conceal these tapes forever also have a chance to buy them.

42

With regard to the legality of the tapes, I live in New Jersey and under our law, it is LEGAL to record telephone conversations if one party to the call allows it. Since I was one party to each call, I authorized it and so the tapes are legal.[26]

Any true American would have to raise an eyebrow and question the very concept of Sean Hannity being "a great American." To be great carries the thought of being far above average in quality, ability, and integrity. And a great American must be trustworthy.

Chapter 3: The Confusion of Entertainment

The subtitle of Glenn Beck's website, www.Glennbeck.com, is "The Fusion of Entertainment and Enlightenment."[1] If you were to tune into Mr. Beck's programs, whether on television, radio, or the Internet (at GBTV.com), you would quickly discern why I dubbed this chapter "The Confusion of Entertainment." Glenn Beck programs are all over the place. His programs are a mixture of comical entertainment, pretentious news reporting, a Sunday afternoon sermon, new world prophecies, and just plain foolishness. On the platform of American conservatism, he has built a very successful, conglomerate business enterprise. It's apparent his audience enjoys being entertained no matter how good or bad the program may be.

At www.GlennBeck.com, in the "About Glenn" section, it reads, "Glenn Beck is one of America's leading multimedia personalities. His quick wit, candid opinions and engaging personality have made The Glenn Beck Program the third-highest-rated radio program in America and GBTV, one of the world's largest streaming video networks. His unique blend of modern-day storytelling and insightful views on current events allowed him to achieve the extraordinary feat of having #1 *New York Times* bestsellers in both fiction and non-fiction. Beck also stars in a live stage show, is the editor of GlennBeck.com and the publisher of TheBlaze.com."[2].

Like his comrades, Rush Limbaugh and Sean Hannity, Mr. Beck is the author of several best-selling books. As of 2010, he has reached the #1 *New York Times* best seller list in four distinct categories: nonfiction, paperback nonfiction, hardcover fiction, and children picture books. His website presents a broad list of books, audiotapes, and other miscellaneous items that can be purchased. Some of his more popular books are *An Inconvenient Book: Real Solutions to the World's Biggest Problems* (2007), *Arguing with Idiots* (2009), *Broke: The Plan to Restore Our Trust,*

44

Truth, and Treasure (2010), and *The Overton Window* (2010), a fictional political thriller. He has also authored the children's book *A Christmas Sweater* (2009) and collaborated with a host of other authors and illustrators on *The Snow Angel* (2011). Lastly, Beck has authored a comic book called *Political Power* (2011).

Many of Glenn Beck's books, although well written, are comically illustrated. For example, on the cover of *Arguing with Idiots*, Beck has a confusing smirk on his face and is dressed in a parody of a military uniform, which some have described as resembling a Nazi or East German military uniform, and the *R* in the word *Arguing* is reversed. As for the cover of his publication *An Inconvenient Book: Real Solutions to the World's Biggest Problems*, Mr. Beck appears on it looking startled or shocked with a torn map of California hanging out of his mouth. On the cover of *Broke: The Plan to Restore Our Trust, Truth, and Treasure*, Beck has a stupid look on his face and is wearing a white T-shirt displaying a patriotic figure whose pockets are hanging out, and Glenn Beck's pockets are likewise hanging out.

Contrary to the title of his book *Broke*, Mr. Beck is far from broke. Not only has he authored, at that time of this writing, seven *New York Times* best-selling publications, but he is also the founder and CEO of Mercury Radio Arts, a multimedia production company that produces content for radio, television, publishing, the stage, and the Internet. As *Forbes* put it, "In his empire there's the ideology——and then there's the money machine."[3] Beck, with his theatrical, comical, controversial, conservative, passionate, and sometime weeping style, has turned himself into a human moneymaking empire, properly named Glenn Beck Inc.

Forbes reported in April 2010 that Beck brings in about $32 million a year by monetizing his mouth.[4] His programs and shows feature Beck talking about politics, constantly criticizing Obama and his administration, and speaking about corrupt government and conspiracy. In addition, he warns of an impending drastic change within our country and on a global scale. Interestingly, in the same

45

Forbes article mentioned earlier, Mr. Beck is quoted as saying, "I could give a flying crap about the political process." Making money, on the other hand, is to be taken very seriously, and controversy is its own coinage. "We're an entertainment company,"[5] he continued.

As a result of Beck's diverse styles of entertainment, he strikes up anger, passion, hatred, division, and fear in his audience. As a devoted Mormon, he often uses Biblical scripture to support his ideology and thoughts. And like his associates, Sean Hannity and Rush Limbaugh, he uses American patriotism and conservative propaganda to promote his message.

I remember listening to Glenn one morning on the radio when he was describing visiting Manhattan's Bryant Park with his family to view an outdoor movie. Glenn Beck told the story of how he and his family, trying to enjoy a movie, became the objects of harassment by some members of the crowd. During the film, he was ridiculed, someone "kicked a cup" of wine on his wife and on his blanket, and another person stood up and yelled, "We hate conservatives here!"

While explaining this incident, Glenn said, "These people were some of the most hateful people I have ever seen…All I wanted to do is go out on a blanket with my family and have dinner in the afternoon sun and sit around Americans, not like-minded Americans, and just watch a movie in the park. And last night at about, when the movie was just about over, my wife and I got out because it was hostile."[6] As he left, some members of the crowd applauded.

On the air Glenn became very emotional, describing the crowd as the "most hateful he has ever seen." He exclaimed that it was "a hostile situation" and he was surprised "that nobody—nobody—in the crowd said 'knock it off. Just, stop. Just be cool. I don't agree with the guy, but just be cool.'" Finally, he concluded, "If I had suggested—and I almost did—wow, does anybody have a rope? Because there's a tree here, you could just lynch me. And I

46

think there would've been a couple in the crowd that would've!"[7]

Although I do not wish anyone to have to experience any kind of harassment, hatefulness, or hostility, I could not help but think that this is exactly how many blacks were treated and made to feel each day in the late 1960s and prior. This treatment was caused by racial prejudices that spewed forth from the same hateful propaganda that Beck and other UMAs pour out over the airwaves each day. So, as it would turn out, Beck and his family got a taste of the poison the UMAs brew.

Glenn Beck is very outspoken; often, he rattles off outrageous and bizarre concepts that even startle his audience. For example, in July 2009, Beck said, while making a guest appearance on the *Fox & Friends* morning show, that "Obama has exposed himself as a person with a deep-seated hatred for white people or the white culture...I'm not saying he doesn't like white people. I'm saying he has a problem. This guy is, I believe, a racist."[8] This type of rhetoric stirs up anger, hatred, and division. In another example of the kinds of barbaric comments coming from Mr. Beck, he responded to the question "what would you do with $50 million?" with the following:

I'm thinking about killing Michael Moore, and I'm wondering if I could kill him myself, or if I would need to hire somebody to do it...No, I think I could. I think he could be looking me in the eye, you know, and I could just be choking the life out. Is this wrong?

For a few brief seconds Beck reflects on the Christian wristband that he use to wear that read "What Would Jesus Do?" and continues...

I stopped wearing my What Would Jesus—band—Do, and I've lost all sense of right and wrong now. I used to be able to say, "Yeah, I'd kill Michael Moore," and then I'd see the little band—What Would Jesus Do? And then I'd realize,

47

"Oh, you wouldn't kill Michael Moore. Or at least you wouldn't choke him to death." And you know, well, I'm not sure.[9]

Here's one last example of Beck's outlandish comments: "When I see a 9/11 victim family on television, or whatever, I'm just like, 'Oh shut up.' I'm so sick of them because they're always complaining."[10]

If this is entertainment, then society's values are deminishing. This popular radio and TV celebrity openly expresses his desire to kill someone, and lack of empathy as if it's the norm. Glenn Beck's ugly mouth is very dangerous because it cultivates the emotions of anger, hatred, fear, and passion. It also sprouts division among the people. Backing his words with Bible verses that he often misapplies, Mr. Beck causes cultlike movement in his believing audience. He claims he is speaking the truth, yet his discussions border on antigovernment gibberish and include talk of conspiracies. In his own words, Beck confesses, "I think I say the things that people are afraid to say—and sometimes the things people are too smart to say…I would take back the things that I say right from the hip, without thinking."[11] His popularity is massive. However, there are just as many people who hate him as there are those who love him. Marketing Evaluations Inc., a company that surveys consumers about their attitudes toward people, brands and characters and turns their responses into what it calls Q Scores. Respondents are first asked whether they recognize the personality or brand, and secondly for those who do, if they have positive or negative feelings for him, her or it. Beck received a positive Q of 17 (those who recognize him) which is above the category average. But his negative Q of 48 (those who had a negative feeling toward him) is practically off the charts. The category average for TV news personalities is a positive Q of 14 and a negative Q of 29.[12]

In June 2010, investigative reporter Alexander Zaitchik released a critical biography titled *Common Nonsense: Glenn Beck and the Triumph of Ignorance*. In an interview about his book, Zaitchik theorized that "Beck's

The Ugly Mouths of America!

politics and his insatiable hunger for money and fame are not mutually exclusive...Beck's true religion is not Patriotism, Mormonism, or Conservatism. His true religion is cross-platform self-marketing...According to Beck's worldview, there's no inherent contradiction between his sophisticated instinct for self-promotion, his propagandist rodeo clown act, his self-image as a media mogul, and his professed belief system. I think he actually believes that God wants him to make a ton of money and become this huge celebrity by fear mongering and generally doing whatever it takes in the media to promote right-wing causes."[13]

On the forty-seventh anniversary of the Reverend Dr. Martin Luther King Jr.'s famous "I Have a Dream" speech in Washington, DC, Glenn Beck held a rally called "Restoring Honor." This rally was held in the exact location of Dr. King's speech, the National Mall. The rally's theme was heavily religious and not overly political. "Something that is beyond man is happening," Beck told his supporters as the rally opened. "America today begins to turn back to God. For too long, this country has wandered in darkness."[14] Among his diverse guests were many Tea Party activists, including featured guest speaker, former Alaska governor, and Republican vice presidential candidate Sarah Palin. Mrs. Palin told the crowd, "It is so humbling to get to be here with you today, patriots—you who are motivated and engaged and concerned, knowing to never retreat. No, we must not fundamentally transform America as some would want; we must restore America and restore her honor."[15]

The crowd was estimated by the event organizers to be around 400,000 to 500,000 people, with another 120,000 watching the event on a dedicated stream on Facebook. However, many news reporters and commentators estimated only approximately 100,000 to 200,000 people in attendance. But, as you now know, the UMAs like to exaggerate things.

Glenn Beck had promoted this event on his radio and television programs. Prior to the event, Beck said, "This is going to be a moment that you'll never be able to paint

49

people as haters, racists, none of it...This is a moment, quite honestly, that I think we reclaim the civil rights movement."[16]

Beck's critics—civil rights leaders, blacks, and others—had vastly different views than he did of the "Restoring Honor" rally. Many felt that the historic date and location of Beck's event tarnished King's memory for the sake of promoting Beck's political agenda. Reverend Al Sharpton, president of the National Action Network and a well-known and powerful civil activist, said of Beck's rally, "When we heard about Glenn Beck, it was puzzling. Because if you read Dr. King's speech, it just doesn't gel with what Mr. Beck or Mrs. Palin are representing."[17] Benjamin Todd Jealous, president of the NAACP, observed of the organizers' request that the crowd not bring any signs, "Dr. King never had to ask anyone to leave their signs and guns at home...To say to your followers, don't bring your signs—it's like saying don't open your mouth."[18]

On that same historic day, Reverend Sharpton was holding a "Reclaim the Dream" rally at the nearby Dunbar High School. At the press conference, Sharpton said, "Dr. King is not owned by blacks. But we can't have different opinions of Dr. King's speech...They're having an antigovernment march on a day King came to appeal to the government. You can't have it both ways."[19]

Although Glenn Beck urged attendees not to bring signs and posters to his event, many of the crowd, who were Tea Party members and mainly white people, did. The most popular image among the items brought was the American flag in its many variations, but many Tea Party shirts, anti-Obama buttons, and Founding Fathers memorabilia were also on hand. As Reverend Sharpton remarked, "Just because you get the spot doesn't mean you are standing up for the dream."[20]

Glenn Beck describes himself as a Mormon whose politics lean toward libertarianism, but he also promotes traditional family values.[21] He has not always been a so-

The Ugly Mouths of America!

called Mormon Christian. Prior to converting to Mormonism, Beck experienced many challenges in his life, including the questionable drowning of his mother in 1979; a divorce from his first wife, Claire Beck, in 1994; and the suicide of his stepbrother. Beck, who had been diagnosed early in his life with attention deficit/hyperactivity disorder (ADHD), has struggled with substance abuse and excessive drinking. As a recovering drug addict and alcoholic, Glenn Beck saw the need to drastically change his life. He did so successfully.

In 1996, Beck attended Yale University and took a class in "Early Christology." Beck then dropped out of college and pursued a radio broadcasting career like his comrades Rush Limbaugh and Sean Hannity. In 1999, Beck married his second wife, Tania, and together they joined the Church of Jesus Christ of Latter-day Saints, the Mormon Christian organization.

As mentioned earlier, Glenn Beck likes to quote Biblical scriptures to support his comments on his radio and television programs. He foretells of coming drastic changes in our society and the world. He predicts these changes will happen soon, perhaps by the 2012 election. The changes include food crises, money crises, a more socialist and perhaps communist government, race riots in the streets, and more. In addition, he says that Hillary Clinton, the current secretary of state, will enter the presidential race and run for president in 2012.[22]

Only time will tell whether any of Glenn Beck's predictions are correct. But I do know from reading God's inspired word that the Bible foretells of coming calamities upon the inhabited Earth (Matthew 24:3-9, 21). I don't necessary agree with Beck on how or when these calamities will come about, but a major change in society on a global scale is destined to eventually happen. I speak more about this subject in chapter seven.

Glenn Beck opposes progressivism. During his 2010 keynote speech to the Conservative Political Action Conference (CPAC), Beck wrote the word "progressivism"

51

on a chalkboard and declared, "This is the disease. This is the disease in America…Progressivism is the cancer in America, and it is eating our Constitution!"[23] For those of us who may be wondering what exactly *progressivism* is, the *Oxford English Dictionary* describes it as "favoring reform or new ideas." If you were to google "what is progressivism?" you would be directed to an organization called Progressive Living. The web address is progressiveliving.org/progressivism.htm. This organization defines progressivism as follows: "Progressivism is a political movement that represents the interests of ordinary people in their roles as taxpayers, consumers, employees, citizens, and parents."[24]

If we combine these two definitions, I cannot see how progressivism could be considered a cancerous disease in America that is eating away at our Constitution at all. Progressivism is, actually, at the very root of the fundamental development of our country. Favoring "reform and new ideas" was the basis upon which thirteen English colonies revolted against Great Britain and eventually formed the United States of America. The Constitution of the United States was written in the interest of having laws that govern and protect "the interests of ordinary people" in the basic roles they take on in everyday living. So if "progressivism is a cancer," as Glenn Beck puts it, then this country was very ill at its beginning.

Progressivism only becomes a problem when—as with anything else—it is taken to the extreme. For example, an organization or individual wants to make a change. The change is reasonable and logical with meaningful benefits for others. In the process of making that change, more ideas and concepts continue to be included, so much so that the original purpose for the change is lost in the multitude of ideas. As a result, there is the blending of the good and bad, the reasonable and foolish, the practical and illogical, so that the progressive desire for change and reform is described as "the far left." The same argument can be made about conservatism: the same scrambling applies, but extreme resistance to change and reform is described as "the far right." This melodramatic "far left" and "far right" schism has become the sickening virus of our society, which I will make more apparent in chapter six, "A House Divided." Like in all other things, there is the necessity to have proper balance.

Joining his peers Rush Limbaugh and Sean Hannity, Glenn Beck attacks President Obama at every opportunity presented. Right or wrong, telling facts or fabrications, this conglomerate trio scrimmages for opportunities to demote the presidency. The attacks by these three UMAs are so numerous that it is difficult to tell who despises the president the most. In addition, because Glenn Beck's speech frequently borders being antigovernmental, and promotes conspiracy theories, the Anti-Defamation League (ADL) have referred to Beck as America's "fearmonger-in-chief". They have also said, "Beck and his guest have made a habit of demonizing President Obama and promoting conspiracy theories about his administration... Beck has even gone so far as to make comparisons between Hitler and Obama and to promote the idea that the president is dangerous."[25]

Like Rush Limbaugh, Beck has mocked the first family. In May 2010, Beck spent over four minutes of airtime making fun of the president's daughter, then eleven-year-old Malia, on his national radio show. To make matters even worse, the mockery also exposed Glenn Beck as a hypocrite. Just a few days before making fun of Malia Obama, while interviewing Sarah Palin, Beck took what appeared to be a principled stand on the matter of respect toward how people should treat the families of public figures. Beck remarked, "Leave my family, leave people's families alone...When it was Bill Clinton, you don't go after Chelsea Clinton. You don't talk about the Bush kids. Now, the minute they get into politics, that's a different story. You leave the families alone."[26] But a day after President Obama had made a comment during a press conference that his daughter Malia had asked him about the BP Gulf oil spill, Mr. Beck, with the support of his cohost Pat Gray, used a falsetto child's voice to make fun of the first family:

53

BECK: (imitating Malia) Daddy? Daddy? Daddy, did you plug the hole yet? Daddy?

PAT GRAY: (imitating Obama) No I didn't, honey.

BECK: (imitating Malia) Daddy, I know you're better than [unintelligible]

GRAY: (imitating Obama) Mm-hmm, big country.

BECK: (imitating Malia) And I was wondering if you've plugged that hole yet.

GRAY: (imitating Obama) Honey, not yet.

BECK: (imitating Malia) Why not, Daddy? But Daddy—

GRAY: (imitating Obama) Not time yet, honey. Hasn't done enough damage.

BECK: (imitating Malia) Daddy?

GRAY: (imitating Obama) Not enough damage yet, honey.

BECK: (imitating Malia) Daddy?

GRAY: (imitating Obama) Yeah?

BECK: (imitating Malia) Why do you hate black people so much?

GRAY: (imitating Obama) I'm part white, honey.

BECK: (imitating Malia) What?

GRAY: (imitating Obama) What?

BECK: (imitating Malia) What'd you say?

GRAY: (imitating Obama) Excuse me?

BECK: (laughing) This is such a ridiculous—this is such a ridiculous thing that his daughter—(imitating Malia) Daddy?

GRAY: It's so stupid.

BECK: How old is his daughter? Like, thirteen?

GRAY: Well, one of them's, I think, thirteen, one's eleven, or something.

BECK: "Did you plug the hole yet, daddy?" Is that's their—that's the level of their education, that they're coming to—they're coming to Daddy and saying "Daddy, did you plug the hole yet?" Plug the hole!

GRAY: (imitating Obama) Yes, I was doing some deep-sea diving yesterday, and—

BECK: (imitating Malia) Daddy?

GRAY: (imitating Obama) Yeah, mm-hmm, mm-hmm, I was doing—

BECK: (imitating Malia) Why—

GRAY: (imitating Obama) Yeah, honey, I'm—

BECK: (imitating Malia) Why, why, why, why, do you still let the polar bears die? Daddy, why do you still let Sarah Palin destroy the environment? Why are—Daddy, why don't you just put her in some sort of a camp?"[27]

This is only a partial transcript of this foolish, grossly disrespectful mockery of the first family, during which Beck attacked the children's level of education. In addition, Glenn Beck and his cohost Pat Gray continued relentlessly with their play, Beck insulting the president by saying, in his childish voice, "Daddy, the best thing you ever did was get that BlackBerry, cause...yeah well, um, I can't, I don't know how to reach you...Daddy, you're a puppet. Did you know that?...I went to a puppet show. Mommy says your presidency is like doing a puppet show." You can get the full spirit of this insulting misuse of air time and listen to the audio in its entirety by googling the words "Glenn Beck smears 11-year old Obama daughter" or visit

55

http://thepoliticalcarnival.net/2010/05/28/audio-glenn-beck-smears-11-year-old-obama-daughter/.

The popularity of this audio clip was tremendous. After playing on the radio, the audio clip went viral, thousands of Internet users listening to it on YouTube and other social and media websites.

There is no doubt that many of Beck's listeners and the public in general were offended that this forty-six-year-old man, a popular media personality, had extensively ridiculed and insulted the president's eleven-year-old daughter on a national radio program. Shortly thereafter, Glenn Beck issued this rather weak apology: "In discussing how President Obama uses children to shield himself from criticism, I broke my own rule about leaving kids out of political debates. The children of public figures should be left on the sidelines. It was a stupid mistake and I apologize—and as a dad I should have known better. "[28] Continuing, he can't help but attack the president for using "children to shield himself from criticism."

The quick infamy earned by these comments and the frequency with which listeners heard them on the Internet must have raised the hairs on Rush Limbaugh's neck. Like an angry hound, he got in the hype and belittled the daughters of the president himself. Only days later, Rush Limbaugh made the following comments on his national radio program with his own version of the falsetto child's voice: "Daddy? Did you shake down BP yet, Daddy? Are you going to make them pay, Daddy?…Did you plug the hole yet, Daddy?"[29] Because Rush Limbaugh's version lacked originality, however, it was not nearly as popular.

All of the attacks on and criticisms of the president and his family from the three amigos are far too many to examine in full in this publication. The reality is that one could compose a 250-page publication on this subject alone, even just by focusing on the three characters of Rush Limbaugh, Sean Hannity, and Glenn Beck. But that is not the main focus of this book. The UMAs' propaganda misleads and divides people. It is often delivered with an undertone of deep disrespect toward the office, organization, person, or subject matter of which they speak. It influences its listeners to imitate this unfavorable, selfish practice of disrespecting others, and it's accomplished under the umbrella of the false pretense of the freedom of speech.

Freedom of speech has its limitations. For example, if in a crowded movie theater or at a public event, one's "freedom of speech" does not give him or her the right to yell "fire" if there is no fire. The reason for this is that it could cause chaos and possibly the serious injury of others. Likewise, on the basis of morals and proper respect, it would be literally wrong to walk up to an elderly lady or a stranger whom you are passing on the street and yell obscenities at her or him for no reason. This would be an abuse of freedom of speech. If you think this logic is incorrect, try yelling obscenities in the face of the next police officer who pulls your vehicle off to the side of the road. You have that right, but imagine how it will work out for you. The UMAs abuse their right to freedom of speech. Dropping all morals and logical thinking, they seriously injure others by showing gross disrespect toward their subjects and also toward their audience, who at times may have an opposing viewpoint. This type of entertainment has made the UMAs very popular in the media as well as filthy rich.

On some rare occasions, sponsors and producers for the programs that feature the Ugly Mouths of America have asked them to tone it down a bit or to back off on a certain subject. Some have threatened to withdraw their sponsorship because of the controversial gibberish and the belittling of public figures and their families. Among the advertisers to pull spots from Glenn Beck's programs are Geico, owned by Warren Buffett's Berkshire Hathaway; ConAgra, Sargento Cheese, Progressive Insurance, Procter & Gamble, the pharmaceutical companies Roche and Sanofi-aventis, and the electronics retailer RadioShack. The sponsors' shifts came after a campaign by ColorOfChange.org, a black political coalition that organized a campaign against the program.[30]Privately held Sargento told its media buyer not to play any of its ads during Beck's

The Ugly Mouths of America!

show. "We market our products to people regardless of their political affiliations," a spokeswoman said. "Yet we do not want to be associated with hateful speech used by either liberal or conservative television hosts."[31] Television advertisers, Coca-Cola, and Walmart have also dissociated themselves from Beck[32]

Beck has also suffered backlash from the many critics of his antigovernment gibberish, conspiracy theories, and prophecies of danger and doom. In early 2011, overall ratings for his radio and television program declined. In March 2011, Buckley Radio yanked Beck from four of its stations after having already pulled him from their flagship station, WOR in New York City, in January. Commenting on the decision to drop the show, Rick Buckley, president of Buckley Radio, said, "In the last six months or so, he has tended to be more and more taking a religious point of view...It didn't do well here in the east. It has not gotten real traction. If you want a religious point of view, we've got plenty of religious stations. You can get it 24/7."[33] According to The New Republic, Glenn's TV show, Glenn Beck, lost more than a million viewers during its 5:00 p.m. slot, going from an average 2.9 million in January 2010 to 1.8 million in January 2011. Analysts suggest viewers and advertisers are tired of his conspiracy theories and related antics. Beck just got to be too much—the tears, the conspiracy theories, and the "Obama is a socialist" drumbeat.[34]

The other two amigos, Rush Limbaugh and Sean Hannity, have also lost some support for their programs. A look at the PPM (Portable People Meter, Arbitron's radio audience measurement system) ratings for the largest talk radio market in the nation bears this out. A comparison of ratings between November 2009 and November 2010 in the New York area shows that Rush Limbaugh's ratings on WABC declined from 5.4 to 5.0. Likewise, year-end to year-end comparisons of the crucial twenty-four to fifty-five demographic show that Rush declined from 3.7 to 2.6 and Sean Hannity and Mark Levin experienced a narrow decline.[35] Hannity was dropped from his Philadelphia radio station along with Beck. Long-time radio executive and

President of *Talk Frontier Media* Randall Bloomquist commented, "There are a lot of program directors whose radio 'spider-sense' is tingling…They're thinking this conservative thing is kind of running its course. We're saying the same things from morning 'til night and yes, we've got a very loyal core audience—but if we ever want to grow, if we want to expand, we've got to be doing more than 18 hours a day of 'Obama is a socialist.'"[36]

Despite falling ratings that apparently began back in January 2010, in August of that year Glenn Beck launched a new website called The Blaze (www.TheBlaze.com). The "about" section on this site reads, "The Blaze is a news, information and opinion site brought to you by a dedicated team of writers, journalists & video producers. Our goal is to post, report and analyze stories of interest on a wide range of topics from politics and culture to faith and family."[37] With regard to The Blaze, Beck said, "There comes a time when you have to stop complaining and do something. And so we decided to hire some actual journalists to launch a new website."[38]According to Beck, the site is intended to give folks a helping hand. "If you are like me, watching the news or reading the paper can be an exercise in exasperation. It's so hard to find a place that helps me make sense of the world I see…We want this to be a place where you can find breaking news, original reporting, insightful opinions, and engaging videos about the stories that matter most." [39]

Like many of Glenn Beck's adventures, TheBlaze.com has faced much criticism. Causing anger with its insulting demeanor, some of its commentary and so-called insightful opinions have turned many off. Political blogger Shel Horowitz writes, "The juxtaposition of 'Glenn Beck' and 'honest source of information' in the same sentence would be amusing, if it weren't scary…The site claims that MLK and the Democratic Party had/have a 'radical leftist agenda,' pays homage to the climate-change deniers, accuses Al Sharpton of racism, and claims that 70 percent of New Yorkers oppose the Ground Zero mosque…a figure I question."[40]

The Ugly Mouths of America!

On September 12, 2011, the day after the ten-year memorial at Ground Zero in New York for the anniversary of the 9/11 terrorist attacks, Glenn Beck launched his new Internet-only broadcasting network GBTV.com. The show's tagline is "The Truth Lives Here." The *Wall Street Journal* reports that the network is set to generate more than $20 million in revenue in its first year.[41] At the time of this writing, GBTV.com has already racked up more than 230,000 paying subscribers. That already eclipses the viewership for the Oprah Winfrey Network.[39] Cost of a subscription is $9.95 per month, and the website offers a fourteen-day free trial. Its advertisements say, "Change the media and you change the world."[42]

In the entertainment world, popularity draws money. It does not matter whether you are liked or disliked, but people seem to enjoy observing someone else's confrontations and problems. Popular so-called newspapers that spread gossip and reality shows that present arguments, hardships, and confrontations have become the norm. Tweeting and blogging have become successful gossiping tools. As a result, many more UMAs have surfaced. They, too, want to their share of the fortune and fame. In the world of political gossip and positioning, the UMAs have become uglier, and many of them have the support of Rush Limbaugh, Sean Hannity, and Glenn Beck.

Chapter 4: The Ugly Gets Uglier

When I started researching the aforementioned radio and television personalities, certain other UMAs—in particular, Dr. Laura Schlessinger, Neal Boortz, and Mark Levin—kept infiltrating into my research. Of these three, Mark Levin has a very close friendship with Sean Hannity, and at times they have expressed their friendship on the air and have also called each other during the broadcasts of their shows.

Unlike the other UMAs, Dr. Laura Schlessinger is being discussed in this publication not because of her conservative talk or her criticism of the president and his administration but mainly because of her hypocrisy. The racist outburst on the airwaves when Dr. Schlessinger was offering an Afro-American woman advice on how to deal with her husband's friends and relatives who made offcolor jokes and remarks regarding her mixed marriage demanded my attention. At its peak, *The Dr. Laura Program* was the second-highest-rated radio show after *The Rush Limbaugh Show* and was heard on more than 450 radio stations.[1] Although I never listen to Dr. Schlessinger's popular radio program, the information I found in my research exposed her as a hypocrite and qualified her as another Ugly Mouth.

As mentioned earlier, on August 10, 2010, Dr. Schlessinger went on a five-minute rant on the air, during which she used the word "nigger" eleven times while speaking to a female caller. The caller phoned into Dr. Schlesinger's radio broadcast to ask for advice on how to deal with her husband's friends and relatives who constantly belittled her. The caller, an Afro-American woman, was married to a Caucasian man. The following is the dialogue that took place between the caller and Dr. Schlessinger as transcribed by Media Matters:

SCHLESSINGER: Jade, welcome to the program.

CALLER: Hi, Dr. Laura.

61

SCHLESSINGER: Hi.

CALLER: I'm having an issue with my husband where I'm starting to grow very resentful of him. I'm black, and he's white. We've been around some of his friends and family members who start making racist comments as if I'm not there or if I'm not black. And my husband ignores those comments, and it hurts my feelings. And he acts like—

SCHLESSINGER: Well, can you give me an example of a racist comment? 'Cause sometimes people are hypersensitive. So tell me what's—give me two good examples of racist comments.

CALLER: OK. Last night—good example—we had a neighbor come over, and this neighbor—when every time he comes over, it's always a black comment. It's, "Oh, well, how do you black people like doing this?" And, "Do black people really like doing that?" And for a long time, I would ignore it. But last night, I got to the point where it—

SCHLESSINGER: I don't think that's racist.

CALLER: Well, the stereotype—

SCHLESSINGER: I don't think that's racist. No, I think that—

CALLER: [unintelligible]

SCHLESSINGER: No, no, no. I think that's—well, listen, without giving much thought, a lot of blacks voted for Obama simply 'cause he was half-black. Didn't matter what he was gonna do in office, it was a black thing. You gotta know that. That's not a surprise. Not everything that somebody says— we had friends over the other day; we got about thirty-five people here—the guys who were gonna start playing basketball. I was going to go out and play basketball. My bodyguard and my dear friend is a black man. And I said, "White men can't jump; I want you on my team." That was racist? That was funny.

The Ugly Mouths of America!

CALLER: How about the N-word? So, the N-word's been thrown around—

SCHLESSINGER: Black guys use it all the time. Turn on HBO, listen to a black comic, and all you hear is nigger, nigger, nigger.

CALLER: That isn't—

SCHLESSINGER: I don't get it. If anybody without enough melanin says it, it's a horrible thing; but when black people say it, it's affectionate. It's very confusing. Don't hang up, I want to talk to you some more. Don't go away.

I'm Dr. Laura Schlessinger. I'll be right back.

[After taking a commercial break, Schlessinger resumed her discussion with the caller.]

SCHLESSINGER: I'm Dr. Laura Schlessinger, talking to Jade. What did you think about during the break, by the way?

CALLER: I was a little caught back by the N-word that you spewed out, I have to be honest with you. But my point is, race relations—

SCHLESSINGER: Oh, then I guess you don't watch HBO or listen to any black comedians.

CALLER: But that doesn't make it right. I mean, race is a [unintelligible]—

SCHLESSINGER: My dear, my dear—

CALLER: —since Obama's been in office—

SCHLESSINGER: —the point I'm trying to make—

CALLER: —racism has come to another level that's unacceptable.

SCHLESSINGER: Yeah. We've got a black man as president, and we have more complaining about racism than ever. I mean, I think that's hilarious.

CALLER: But I think, honestly, because there's more white people afraid of a black man taking over the nation.

SCHLESSINGER: They're afraid.

CALLER: If you want to be honest about it [unintelligible]

SCHLESSINGER: Dear, they voted him in. Only 12 percent of the population's black. Whites voted him in.

CALLER: It was the younger generation that did it. It wasn't the older white people who did it.

SCHLESSINGER: Oh, OK.

CALLER: It was the younger generation—

SCHLESSINGER: All right. All right.

CALLER: —that did it.

SCHLESSINGER: Chip on your shoulder. I can't do much about that.

CALLER: It's not like that.

SCHLESSINGER: Yeah. I think you have too much sensitivity—

CALLER: So it's OK to say "nigger"?

The Ugly Mouths of America!

SCHLESSINGER: —and not enough sense of humor.

CALLER: It's OK to say that word?

SCHLESSINGER: It depends how it's said.

CALLER: Is it OK to say that word? Is it ever OK to say that word?

SCHLESSINGER: It's—it depends how it's said. Black guys talking to each other seem to think it's OK.

CALLER: But you're not black. They're not black. My husband is white.

SCHLESSINGER: Oh, I see. So, a word is restricted to race. Got it. Can't do much about that.

CALLER: I can't believe someone like you is on the radio spewing out the "nigger" word, and I hope everybody heard it.

SCHLESSINGER: I didn't spew out the "nigger" word.

CALLER: You said, "Nigger, nigger, nigger."

SCHLESSINGER: Right, I said that's what you hear.

CALLER: Everybody heard it.

SCHLESSINGER: Yes, they did.

CALLER: I hope everybody heard it.

SCHLESSINGER: They did, and I'll say it again—

CALLER: So what makes it OK for you to say the word?

SCHLESSINGER: —nigger, nigger, nigger is what you hear on HB—

CALLER: So what makes it—

SCHLESSINGER: Why don't you let me finish a sentence?

CALLER: OK.

SCHLESSINGER: Don't take things out of context. Don't double N—NAACP me. Tape the—

CALLER: I know what the NAACP—

SCHLESSINGER: Leave them in context.

CALLER: I know what the N-word means and I know it came from a white person. And I know the white person made it bad.

SCHLESSINGER: All right. Thank you very much. Thank you very much. Can't have this argument. You know what? If you're that hypersensitive about color and don't have a sense of humor, don't marry out of your race. If you're going to marry out of your race, people are going to say, "OK, what do blacks think? What do whites think? What do Jews think? What do Catholics think?" Of course there isn't a one-think per se. But in general there's "think."

And what I just heard from Jade is a lot of what I hear from black-think—and it's really distressing [sic] and disturbing. And to put it in its context, she said the N-word, and I said, on HBO, listening to black comics, you hear "nigger, nigger, nigger." I didn't call anybody a nigger. Nice try, Jade. Actually, sucky try.

Need a sense of humor, sense of humor—and answer the question. When somebody says, "What do blacks think?" say, "This is what I think. This is what I read that if you take a

The Ugly Mouths of America!

poll the majority of blacks think this." Answer the question and discuss the issue. It's like we can't discuss anything without saying there's -isms?

We have to be able to discuss these things. We're people—goodness gracious me. Ah—hypersensitivity, OK, which is being bred by black activists. I really thought that once we had a black president, the attempt to demonize whites hating blacks would stop, but it seems to have grown, and I don't get it. Yes, I do. It's all about power. I do get it. It's all about power and that's sad because what should be in power is not power or righteousness to do good—that should be the greatest power.[2]

Dr. Schlessinger makes some interesting comments regarding the use of the word "nigger." As a black man raised during the 1960s and 1970s in a predominantly black neighborhood on the south side of Chicago, I have always been offended by this word. As Dr. Schlessinger acknowledge, as if it's OK, that black guys make use of it quite often when talking to each other. To be more accurate, some blacks do, but the ones I choose to associate with do not. Many of us, especially those who are mature, educated, and understand the struggles of our parents and grandparents, take offense to the use of the word "nigger." We also understand the "demeanor" of the word. We find it derogative. It doesn't matter whether it is a black person using the word "nigger" or some other race; in nearly every situation, "nigger" is a bad choice from the English vocabulary.

Among young people today, I have heard Hispanics, whites, and blacks use the N-word when conversing with each other. In addition, the young men called themselves "dogs" or "dawgs," and the young ladies refer to themselves as "bitches." I am offended by this. However, I recognize their ignorance. This is what society has taught them through the stereotyping of what it means to be "cool," "tough," "hip," and such. We see it displayed in the popular movies of our day and the music of our hip-hop, rap, and rock artists. Many of our youth have been influenced by a culture so sullied

67

with foolishness and unclean speech that they cannot distinguish reality from fantasy, proper from improper, or intelligent from unintelligent. They become victims of gross entertainment. This principle proves true: what you feed the eyes and the ears, the mind retains and believes. As a result, they choose other offensive words, including profanity and in some cases a combination of gross profanity and slang, to emotionalize or emphasize a subject or to enhance a joke. This does not make the use of inglorious foul language morally correct. Those who use such language often display it on t-shirts or hats to draw attention to themselves, it acceptable to them, but offensive to others. Dr. Laura Schlessinger said, "I don't get it…It is confusing"; perhaps to her it is, and that's a strong enough reason for why she should refrain from using or counseling someone on the use of the word "nigger."

Dr. Schlessinger added, "Some black comedians use the word all the time…" At least when performing, they might. In the seventies and eighties, there were some black comedians, such as Redd Foxx, Richard Pryor, and Eddie Murphy, who made their living using the word "nigger." However, its use was often associated with the ignorant or uneducated black character of their comical scripts. In this theatrical domain, the comic often associated the N-word with the white dominance or attitude of superiority over the poor black man or woman. Even in that time period, as well as today, many blacks found and find this "stereotype humor" not so humorous or entertaining.

A white person using the N-word and directing it toward a black is similar to a black person calling a white person a "honky." It's inappropriate and a bad choice of word in the English language. The same can be said of other offensive names for stereotypes, such as "faggot," "redneck," "spook," "hymie," "coon," "chink," and many more. As a professional counselor, Dr. Schlessinger should have known better.

Maybe Dr. Laura Schlessinger was confused due to the fact that she is neither a medical doctor nor a

68

psychologist. Her PhD is in physiology—a degree that has nothing to do with interpersonal relations. Critics of her show point out the questionable ethics of using a degree in one field to imply credibility in another; arguing that in and of itself could be viewed as morally wrong.[3] After she began dispensing personal advice on the radio, she earned a postdoctoral certification in marriage, family, and child counseling from the University of Southern California.[4]

Dr. Schlessinger is best known for her no-nonsense philosophy of personal responsibility and self-motivation. She emphasizes moral messages, such as no sex outside of marriage, moms shouldn't work, divorce is wrong, abortion is wrong, living together without marriage is wrong, marriage too young is wrong, marriage without children is hardly a marriage at all, homosexuality is destructive and in her words "a biological error", gay marriage is wrong, girls should not dress like "sluts", and the family unit is of paramount importance.[5] She has authored several books, including *Ten Stupid Things Women Do To Mess Up Their Lives* (1994), *How Could You Do That?! The Abdication of Character, Courage, and Conscience* (1996), *Ten Stupid Things Men Do To Mess Up Their Lives* (1997), *The Proper Care and Feeding of Husbands* (2004), *Woman Power: Transform Your Man, Your Marriage* (2004).

Her website, Drlaura.com, says in its "about" section, "As one of the most popular talk show hosts in radio history, Dr. Laura Schlessinger offers no-nonsense advice infused with a strong sense of ethics, accountability, and personal responsibility; she's been doing it successfully for more than 30 years, reaching approximately 9 million listeners weekly."[6] According to CNN.com, her audience was made up of "people who looked to Dr. Laura to set them straight in their relationships, ethical disputes and moral conundrums."[7] Dr. Laura has given much advice over the past thirty years on family values that she has apparently struggled to uphold.

Schlessinger married when she was twenty-five and had at least two extramarital affairs before she got divorced

69

from her first husband. Her first known extramarital affair was with Bill Ballance, a radio talk show host broadcast from Los Angeles.[8] Dr. Schlessinger had another extramarital affair with Lewis G. Bishop, a professor of neuron physiology. During that time Professor Bishop was also married. After divorcing their spouses, they lived together for nine years and eventually married in 1985.[9]

Her family has not been a positive example to society but has mirrored many of the dysfunctional and broken homes that are so prevalent in society today. She describes her childhood as "difficult" due to the rocky, "unloving" marriage between her father, a Jewish US citizen, and her mother, an Italian Catholic.[10] She has described her father as "petty, insensitive, mean, thoughtless, demeaning and downright unloving." She described her mother as a person with "pathological pride" and who "was never grateful," who "would always find something to criticize," and who "constantly expressed disdain for men, sex and love." [11] As a result of these things, Dr. Schlessinger never got along well with her father, and she and her mother had been estranged for at least the fourteen years before her mother's death in 2002. Schlessinger has also been estranged from her sister since the mid-1970s. She has reportedly told listeners, "I love shunning…It reminds people they have an obligation to others."[12]

In October 1998, nude photos of Dr. Schlessinger surfaced on the Internet. One of the photos displayed her sitting with her legs spread wide apart. At first, Schlessinger denied the photos, stating that it was a different woman. Eventually, after finally admitting that she was the woman in the pictures, she filed a lawsuit claiming invasion of privacy and copyright violation. In 1999, the court ruled that Schlessinger did not own the rights to the photos. Schlessinger's explanation to her audience was that she was embarrassed but that the photos were taken when she was going through a divorce and had "no moral authority."[13]

The nude photos of Dr. Schlessinger were taken by her first publicly exposed extramarital affair partner, Bill

70

Ballance. When asked why he posted the pictures, Ballance replied,

The fact is, she has been stealing my material for so many years. The fact is, she told so many lies about our relationship, an example being our being together just a week or two, and that she was on my show just a few days, or a few times rather. She was on my show for two and a half years. We went together for a torrid two and a half years. I'm tired of being lied about and the longer it goes on the more people believe her. They'll think I'm the interloper. People will begin to assume that I was the beginner and that she taught me everything I know.[14]

In our youth, we all have no doubt done or said things at one time or another that were hypocritical or went against our personal beliefs. Perhaps we have given into dares, challenges from our peers, or thrills that excite us at that moment in time. But what makes you a hypocrite is when you continue in a behavior or practice over an extended period of time so that your hypocrisy becomes a part of your character. As a result of trying to hide this flawed feature of your personality or character, you present a false pretense of being someone else or pretending it does not exist. In the case of Dr. Schlessinger, CNN.com expressed it best: "...her determination to act as America's conscience often put her at odds with critics, who were quick to question Schlessinger's own life decisions."[15] As a popular public figure who gives counsel on marriage, family life, and family values, she should be exemplary in practicing what she preaches.

Another Ugly Mouth is Neal Boortz. His national syndicated radio program, *The Neal Boortz Show*, is broadcast throughout the country and has nearly six million listeners each week.[16] If you were to visit his website, www.boortz.com, you would find that it says Boortz is the "Talk Master," the "Mighty Whitey," and the "High Priest of the Church of the Painful Truth."[17] Just the reference to himself as the "Mighty Whitey" should tell us something about his character. Boortz often plays the race card when

71

simplifying his ideological views and his discriminating insight. I would go on record, after listening to Neal Boortz for over two years, as saying that it appears that he is a racist and takes pleasure in making racist comments that cause controversy and are offensive to his audience. Of course, these tactics keep his name in the media and keep the revenue coming in. Neal is a confirmed Libertarian. He believes that the principal difference between the Democrats and the Republicans is that the Democrats just want to grow our Imperial Federal Government and spend money just a bit faster than the Republicans do.[18]

In August 2005, the United States was hit by one of the most powerful and deadliest hurricanes in US history. Hurricane Katrina had struck the Gulf Coast from central Florida all the way to Texas. The most significant number of deaths occurred in New Orleans and Louisiana, with a total death count in this area of over 1800 people.[19] Property damage was estimated to be over $75 billion, and many people were left without homes and the basic necessities for life.[20]

In reporting the devastating outcome of the blow suffered by New Orleans from Hurricane Katrina, The *New York Times* editorialized that "it is not a coincidence that many of those hard-hit, low-lying areas have had poor and predominantly African-American residents."[21] *USA Today* reported that "the low-lying wards that suffered the worst damage were mostly black neighborhoods."[22] Editors of the journal *World Watch* drew attention to the article "Race and the High Ground in New Orleans" with the subheadline "Poor and black = low, wet, and maybe dead."[23] African-Americans made up 67 percent of New Orleans's pre-Katrina population and over 74 percent of its flood victims, whites made up nearly 20 percent of the victims, and Hispanics and Asians made up 3 percent of the victims each.[24]

Of those actually killed by the storm, African-American victims outnumbered white victims by more than double: they comprised 66 percent of the storm deaths in New Orleans, while whites made up 31 percent. This is fairly

72

proportionate to the relative population of New Orleans pre-storm.[25]

On the January 30, 2008, edition of his nationally syndicated radio show, Neal Boortz described the city of New Orleans as having been, prior to Hurricane Katrina, "a city of parasites, a city of people who could not and had no desire to fend for themselves." During the show, Boortz said, "When these Katrina so-called refugees were scattered about the country, it was just a glorified episode of putting out the garbage."[26] When reading from the Associated Press report on Senator John Edwards's withdrawal from the 2008 presidential race, Boortz made the following comments:

I like this: "Edwards's campaign will end the way it began thirteen months ago, with the candidate pitching in to rebuild lives in a city still ravaged by Hurricane Katrina. Edwards embraced New Orleans as a glaring symbol of what he described as a Washington that didn't hear the cries of the downtrodden." Cries of the downtrodden, my left butt cheek. That wasn't the cries of the downtrodden; that's the cries of the useless, the worthless. New Orleans was a welfare city, a city of parasites, a city of people who could not and had no desire to fend for themselves. You have a hurricane descending on them and they sit on their fat asses and wait for somebody else to come rescue them. "It's somebody else's job to get me out of here. It's somebody else's job to save my life. Not mine. Send me a bus, send me a limo, send me a boat, send me a helicopter, send me a taxi, send me something. But you certainly don't expect me to actually work to get myself out of this situation, do you? Haven't you been watching me for generations? I've never done anything to improve my own lot in life. I've never done anything to rescue myself. Why do you expect me to do that now, just because a levee broke?"

And then Edwards said, yeah, it was Washington's problem, it was all Washington's problem, it was all George Bush's fault. You had a city of parasites and leeches, and that's George Bush's fault? So, boy, I need to slow down. I'm saying too many of the things I actually believe today.[27]

73

Later, when President Obama said "his administration remains focused on rebuilding New Orleans and the Gulf Coast" and expressed that anything less "would be a betrayal of who we are as a country,"[28] Neal Boortz had an opposing view. He tweeted, "Obama wants to rebuild New Orleans. Why? Build it and they will come."[29] The "they" he was referring to in his tweet was human debris. Boortz describes the Katrina refugees as "debris" having washed across the country and Katrina as having cleansed New Orleans and as having washed out that debris.[30] This UMA is an advocate of hatred and racism.

When commenting on the amount of carjackings and graffiti being sprayed in Atlanta, Neal Boortz went on another all-out attack with the following destructive, racist verbiage:

You know what? I, for one, am tired of putting up with this crap. And you want to know why I moved out of Atlanta and only spend a couple of weeks a year in this town? That's one of the reasons. Carjackings, violence, people getting shot. It's ridiculous. This city harbors an urban culture of violence. And I want you to look around. You drive into the city. The railroad overpass is on the downtown connector covered with graffiti. And that—that is just an advertisement for everybody coming into this town that we really don't give a damn about those who would screw up our quality of life around here. We really just don't care. We don't care enough to paint over graffiti on the overpasses that come into our city, advertising welcome to Atlanta, here's some of our finest graffiti, from some of our finest urban thugs and their little gang signs. And pick up the paper tomorrow morning. Read about all the carjackings. Read about the innocent people shot for the pure de-hell of it.

This town is starting to look like a garbage heap. And we got too damn many urban thugs, yo, ruining the quality of life for everybody. And I'll tell you what it's gonna take. You people, you are—you need to have a gun. You need to have training. You need to know how to use that gun. You need to get a permit to carry that gun. And you do in fact need to carry that gun and we need to see some dead thugs littering

74

the landscape in Atlanta. We need to see the next guy that tries to carjack you shot dead right where he stands. We need more dead thugs in this city. And let their—let their mommas—let their mommas say, "He was a good boy. He just fell in with the good crowd." And then lock her ass up.[31]

Afterward, in June 2011, MSNBC television host Ed Schultz expressed his concerns about the right-wing rhetoric that has become so popular on the airwaves. Schultz said, "There's something very ugly and dangerous going on in this country…Right-wing talk show hosts seem to be amping up racist and reckless rhetoric like never before…the level of racist and violent rhetoric on hard right-wing radio today is off the charts."Schultz continued, explaining that Boortz "just advocated murder in the streets of Atlanta" and guessing that "Neal wasn't thinking of white thugs." Schultz also called Boortz "reckless, stupid and a racist."[32]

These are just a few examples of the outrageous, racist, and violent rhetoric that spews from the mouth of Mr. Boortz. By referring to himself, furthermore, as the "Mouth of the South," the "Talk Master," and "Mighty Whitey," Boortz reveals a powerfully racial undertone to his character and his message. When blacks call into his radio program, Boortz changes his voice to depict a southern white master or the ignorant slang of the Deep South Negro of old. The website www.wsbradio.com refers to Boortz as "full of irresistible wisecracks and irrefutable libertarian wisdom…"[33] I'd like to finish by saying he's just full of it.

You may wonder, if Neal Boortz is a racist talk master, why is he still on the air? The answer is simple: because this is what sells. Boortz has received many industry accolades, including being named one of the "25 Most Important Radio Talk Show Hosts in America" by *Talkers Magazine* and one of "Georgia's 100 Most Influential People" by *Georgia Trend*.[34] With over six million listeners to his radio program, Boortz's influence has become very dangerous. Ed Schultz put it bluntly by saying, "The level of open racism by right-wing talkers I think is obscene. We're not talking about name-calling here. Where's the pushback?

75

Where's the accountability? Where's the responsibility?"[35] This is stunning. Boortz promotes violence, unlawful behavior, and even the taking of arms and killing in the streets. As Vice President of the NAACP Hilary Shelton Sr said, "What we just heard was the clinical definition of racism. Racism with prejudice plus power! There is no more power that we have than to take someone else's life. When you have someone who is actually advocating the taking of African-Americans, and so thinly veiled, no one should miss exactly the stereotype again he brought into this conversation. Using terms like 'yo,' talking about 'urban hood,' those kinds of issues, we know that he is talking about African-Americans. We know he's telling white Americans they should buy guns and shoot them and that will somehow solve a problem."[36]

The ugly talk of racism does not solve problems but only creates bigger ones. It inflames a society of hatred and is extremely divisive. Neal Boortz is a problem.

And then we have Mark Levine. Mr. Levine is a close friend of Rush Limbaugh and Sean Hannity. He has been a frequent guest and a substitute host on *The Sean Hannity Show* and has also been an advisor to Rush Limbaugh. Limbaugh frequently refers to him on the air as "F. Lee Levin" a tongue-in-cheek reference to the famous defense attorney F. Lee Bailey. However, he is more well-known by his nickname "The Great One," coined by Sean Hannity.

Of the three UMAs mentioned in this chapter, as well as all the other UMAs named in this publication, I would venture to say that Mark Levin is probably the most educated, most intelligent, and most respected. He currently practices law in the private sector, heading up the prestigious Landmark Legal Foundation in Washington, DC. In addition, Levin served as a top advisor to several members of President Ronald Reagan's cabinet, including as chief of staff to the attorney general of the United States.[37] However, in my humble opinion, "The Great One" he is not.

The Ugly Mouths of America!

Although this self-righteous title of "The Great One" was given to Mark Levin by so-called Great American Sean Hannity, for him to accept it indicates a measure of arrogance and haughtiness in his character. If you are a Bible reader, you may recall that when someone called Christ Jesus "good," Christ responded, "Why do you call me good? No one is good except one, God" (Luke 18:19).

I must admit that I debated whether to include Mark Levin in this publication, but the decisive factors were his condescending speech and the excessive name-calling he yells across the radio waves. These things clearly indicate that Levin, to an extent, really believes he is "The Great One." There is no doubt that Mark Levin, a lawyer, advisor, and expert in constitutional law, is a highly educated man. But he is also proud, haughty, arrogant, disrespectful, and outspoken. He fits in well with the other UMAs.

Because of his unrighteous arrogance, Mr. Levin speaks down condescendingly to his listening audience. When callers phone in to his radio program, he insults their intelligence and comprehension. If a caller disagrees with Mark Levin, he calls them names like "idiot," "smock," "moron," and worse, totally disgracing the caller on the air. He also uses this type of verbiage when speaking about the president of the United States and other prominent individuals. This method of entertainment, educating, and distributing information teaches that it is OK to disrespect and mimic others as well as engage in childish name-calling. He often ascribes sexually offensive titles to important figures. For example, Mark Levin refers to Richard Durbin as "Little Dick Durbin," Bill Clinton as "BJ," Hillary Clinton as "Her Thighness," Anthony Weiner as "Anthony's Weiner," and the National Organization for Women as "the National Organization for Really Ugly Women."[39] He has also referred to Jesse Jackson as "Jesse Jerkson," Al Sharpton as "Al Not so Sharpton," David Letterman as "the Buck-toothed Moron," Donald Trump as "Donald Chump," Al Franken as "the Spiteful Troll," Nancy Pelosi as "Stretch," Joe Biden as "Plugs," and President Obama as "Milhaus."[38] This list could go on and on because this is the foolishness that sells.

I have an experience that I would like to share. It happened one evening while I was leaving a shopping mall. I heard a father yelling at his son, who was only five or six years old. I was parked next to the man's vehicle and was getting back into my car after having finished shopping. The father grabbed his son by the arm and yelled at him, calling him a "moron and an idiot" and saying "don't you ever do that again!" The child started crying from emotional embarrassment, fear, and possibly a bruised arm. I sat in my car for a few minutes, thinking perhaps the child may have run out into the parking lot and had scared or frightened his dad by nearly getting hit by a moving vehicle. Then I reflected on my childhood and thought about how, when I was a child, my father had never spoken to me that way regardless of what childish or foolish mistakes I may have made. But then again, my father had never listened to Mark Levin. I don't know if this man ever listened to Levin either, but it is this type of insulting, degrading communication spewed over the airwaves telling society it's ok. What ever happen to becoming a positive role model for your family and society?

The Ugly Mouths of America!

Chapter 5: It's Tea Time!

I had known nothing about the Tea Party movement other than what history has taught me regarding the Boston Tea Party of 1773. The Tea Party movement of the past was a protest by colonists who opposed the British tax on tea. The colonists demonstrated their rejection of the tax by dumping British tea overboard from the dock ships in the harbor. In my research, I've learned that the Tea Party theme has been used throughout history by antitax protesters. However, shortly after the election of our first Afro-American president, Barack H. Obama, a new, modern-day Tea Party movement materialized in protest (it appears) of nearly all of Obama's administrative policies and procedures. It has become teatime: the impetuous establishment of a new, white-majority political force that is in opposition to the Obama administration has begun.

The modern-day Tea Party Movement has several prominent figures in its membership, including Rush Limbaugh, former vice presidential nominee Sarah Palin, Sean Hannity, Glenn Beck, Neal Boortz, Mark Levin, and Michelle Bachmann.

On September 12, 2009, just eight months after Obama's inauguration, the modern-day Tea Party movement held its first major national march in Washington, DC. A massive crowd of approximately seventy-five thousand people[1] gathered to march from the Freedom Plaza to the steps of the Capitol Building. The event was organized and strongly promoted by UMA Glenn Beck as the "9/12 March." Although Mr. Beck named the march, he did not take ownership of it. Beck described his role in the organizational march with the following: "If you build it, they will come."[2] Beck calls on us to return to the unity that we formed as a nation the day after the 9/11 terrorist attacks on America. During that time, we were united as Americans; it did not matter who was in the Oval Office, and we supported the president in his declaration of the war on terrorism.

79

This time, however, the unity was different. In the article "American Grotesque," John Jeremiah Sullivan, a white American writer and editor, describes the 9/12 March this way: "For the first time in our history, a black man lives in the White House, and today's is the first massive protest against his administration, and 99.9999 percent of us are white and fan-followers of race baiting pundits [UMAs] and mind you, this is in America, where you can't walk into a convenience store without having or witnessing at least three intense, awkward, occasionally inspiring moments of racial tension—but despite all of that, today has 'nothing to do with race.' This phenomenon will be known to future Americans as 'the Race Miracle of 9/12.'"[3]

In reality, did this march have anything to do with race? Were the Tea Party goers in opposition to having a black man in the White House and to the thought of a black family being honored as the first family? John Sullivan continues by describing his observations of the participants of this protest march:

There is definitely overt racism here. Later you'll hear there wasn't, but it's just strangely coded. Perhaps owing to the advanced age of many of us—the same factor, in other words, that caused the tea-bagging embarrassment—we still revert to seventies soul-brother jive talk when we want to be racist. The YES I AM pimp king is one example, but there are plenty of others. A sign shows Obama digging a grave for the Constitution, with the caption I DON'T DIG BARACK. That's too subtle to serve as a convincing example, maybe, but another man holds a sign that reads HEY, BRO, HANDS OFF MY WALLET, next to a picture of a monkey's face. You start to see.

A father and a little boy standing by a tree. Father's sign reads WE KNOW HE SNEAKS CIGARETTES BUT SERIOUSLY IS THE PRESIDENT STILL SMOKING CRACK?[4]

This well-written article by John Sullivan helps us to comprehend the so-called grassroots of the Tea Party

The Ugly Mouths of America!

movement. He further describes other signs held by the participants of the 9/12 March:

Standing on a garbage can and commanding a lot of attention is a strange figure. A small man or woman—you can't see enough of its body to tell—holds a handmade sign that reads YES I AM. The creature wears an Obama mask. When people holler "Obama!" it looks in their direction and does a little shuffle. Atop the Obama mask sits a fake gold crown. Obama thinks he's a king! (Is that what YES I AM means? Yes, I am a king?) The king has on a bright purple pimp's coat with faux-leopard-skin trim. An African king? It looks like something you'd see and turn away from in a southern antiques shop. We do turn away, after taking a pic.[5]

John Jeremiah Sullivan names his article "American Grotesque," and just so we are all crystal clear on what we are discussing, *grotesque* means ugly and distorted. There is an ugly face to the modern-day Tea Party movement. Publisher of *The Washington Note* Steve Clemons wrote, "But after reading John Jeremiah Sullivan's new article in *GQ*, 'American Grotesque,' I think 'grotesque nationalism' may fit just as well as 'pugnacious nationalism.'"[6] So what is *pugnacious*? It means simply *quick to argue and fight*. This is a growing problem that has resurfaced in America. It is an ugly, distorted opinion that is ready to argue and fight for its cause.

On July 13, 2010, the NAACP passed a resolution to condemn extremist elements within the Tea Party, calling on Tea Party leaders to repudiate those in their ranks who use racist language in their signs and speeches. According to www.NAACP.org,

The resolution came after a year of high-profile media coverage of attendees of Tea Party marches using vile, antagonistic racial slurs & images. In March, respected members of the Congressional Black Caucus reported that racial epithets were hurled at them as they passed by a Washington, DC, health care protest. Civil rights legend John Lewis was called the "n-word" in the incident while others in the crowd used ugly anti-gay slurs to describe

81

Congressman Barney Frank, a long-time NAACP supporter and the nation's first openly gay member of Congress.

Missouri Representative Emmanuel Cleaver was spat on during the incident, and so it was particularly appropriate that the resolution was passed as NAACP delegates gathered in Kansas City for our 101st Annual Convention.[7]

NAACP President Benjamin Todd Jealous said in a written statement announcing the unanimous vote, "What we take issue with is the Tea Party's continued tolerance for bigotry and bigoted statements...The time has come for them to accept the responsibility that comes with influence and make clear there is no place for racism and anti-Semitism, homophobia and other forms of bigotry in their movement."[8]

Of course, this was followed by animosity and a war of words between Tea Partiers and prominent leaders of the NAACP. In the article "War of Words between NAACP, Tea Party Escalates," Liz Goodwin writes:

Tea Party activists quickly shot back, calling the NAACP racist and irrelevant. "It's a little ironic that an organization that has lost legitimacy through its own racism is trying to call another racist," Mark Meckler of Tea Party Patriots told the L.A. Times.

Tea Party Express' Williams went farther in an interview with NPR flagged by Talking Points Memo. "We are dealing with people who are professional race-baiters who make a very good living off this kind of thing. They make more money off of race than any slave trader, ever," he said. "It's time groups like the NAACP went to the trash heap of history where they belong along with all the other vile, racist groups that emerged in our history." On CNN, he called the group "a bunch of old fossils looking to make a buck off skin color."

Dallas Tea Party founder Phillip Dennis said on FOX that the NAACP is "irrelevant" and should have ended 50 years ago.

The Ugly Mouths of America!

Republican National Committee Chairman Michael Steele said the NAACP should stop "name calling."

Many condemned the tea party's attack on the civil rights group as wrong-headed.[9]

So I deemed it wise to take a look at the Tea Party's founders and origins, and I endeavored to determine the inner motives that drive this organization. Taking a look at its beginnings, three key names are found: a conservative blogger from Seattle, Keri Carender; senator, presidential-wannabe, and liberal Ron Paul; and the extremely wealthy Koch brothers, David and Charles Koch.

In February 2009, Keri Carender organized a protest against President Obama's signing of a stimulus bill into law. She called her protest a "porkulus protest." The word 'porkulus' refers to a group of people in the government who try to enact policy that will take the wealth away from the American people. Her protest was formed without any support from outside groups, and approximately 120 people participated. Carender contacted Fox News contributor and conservative author Michelle Malkin, and Malkin publicized the protest in her blog. Later that same month, Carender organized a second protest rally, which over two hundred people attended. Although the term "Tea Party" was not used to describe the rally, some Tea Party leaders credit Keri Carender for the movement's first organized rally.

Second, we have the Libertarian Ron Paul. In an article published by *The American Business Journal* entitled "Tea Party Patriots: The Ron Paul Revolution," Paul is described as follows: "Though the Tea Party Patriots has no official leader or affiliation to the Grand Old Party, much of the political philosophy is relatable. Boston-based political science and foreign affairs magazine The Atlantic has dubbed 76-year-old Paul the 'intellectual godfather' of the Tea Party movement and the Tea Party Patriots. Knowing Paul's political history, and political beliefs, it's a valid stance."[10]

83

In 1976, Ron Paul founded the Foundation for Rational Economics and Education. This organization published several newsletters under Ron Paul's name that claimed over one hundred thousand readers. One of those newsletters, *The New Republic*, was noted for its vile racism, homophobia, and persistence in spreading conspiracy theories. Popular subjects of *The New Republic* newsletters included warnings of "a coming race war" and "the federal-homosexual cover up on AIDS." The September 1992 *Political Report* warned "every honest American should be armed" to prepare for the coming violence. It also included the following: "Today, gangs of young blacks bust into a bank lobby firing rounds at the ceiling...We don't think a child of 13 should be held as responsible as a man of 23. That's true for most people, but black males age 13 who have been raised on the streets and who have joined criminal gangs are as big, strong, tough, scary and culpable as any adult, and should be treated as such." [11]In addition, contributing editor for *The New Republic* notes a few more selections from the Ron Paul newsletters:

The June 1990 Political Report carried an item entitled, "Race War?" which claimed that war was on the horizon because of "the victimization mentality created by the civil rights movement, where every black failure is a white crime.[12]

The August 1990 Political Report claimed that "we've got a potential race war."[13]

The December 1990 Investment Letter reported that "Abortion is rampant, race war is heating up, AIDS is spreading, and inflation is wiping out the middle class." [14]

A January 1993 Survival Report item headlined "Poor Marge Schott!" defended the former Cincinnati Reds owner, who was "being crucified" after she referred to her own players as "million dollar niggers," said that "sneaky goddamn Jews are all alike" and "only fruits wear earrings," and claimed that Hitler was an initially positive force for Germany.[15]

84

In June 1994 Survival Report—two months after South Africa's first democratic election—an item headlined, "There Goes South Africa," claimed that "Mandela is trying to appear as a moderate, and indeed he may be as the Red ANC goes." The newsletter advocated a separate state for whites in South Africa, writing, "If everyone accepts the notion that a homeland can be created for the Palestinians, I wonder why no consideration is given by world opinion leaders to a similar situation for the whites in South Africa, as they have requested."[16]

The August 1991 issue of the Political Report claimed that George H.W. "Bush wanted a war, for Rockefeller oil and New World Order purposes, and snookered [Saddam] Hussein into it."[17]

The February 1994 Survival Report addressed "the supposed suicide of Vince Foster," and in an item entitled "Murderous Clintonians" from the August 1994 issue, the newsletter claimed, "But let's just say [Independent Counsel Robert Fiske] had discovered evidence of a White House conspiracy to kill [Deputy White House Counsel Vince] Foster and cover it up. Would he have revealed it?" It also wrote of "the decade-long adulterous affair between Hillary Clinton and Vince Foster."[18]

The November 1994 issue of the Survival Report celebrated anti-government militias in an item entitled, "Why Militias Scare the Striped Pants Off Big Government." Evoking the American Revolution, the newsletter declared, "These are the times that try men's souls," and concluded that the rising militia movement "is an encouraging sign that the end of government as we know it may be near." That issue also sold something called the "Ron Paul Privacy Card."[19]

The June 1993 Survival Report, on claims that David Koresh had molested a young girl, said, "How dare the Clinton administration talk about sexual deviance? Its officials could have had their own float in the Gay, Lesbian, and Bisexual Parade."[20]

The Ugly Mouths of America!

The November 1993 Survival Report referred to people with AIDS who visit dentists as "deadly customers" and complained that "the criminal 'Justice' Department wants to force dentists to treat these Darth Vader types under the vicious Americans With Disabilities Act." The newsletter goes on to claim, "we all have the right to discriminate, which is what freedom of association is all about, especially against killers."[21]

The "brain" behind these newsletters, which bear his name, is Ron Paul. However, when seeking the Republican presidential nomination in 2012, Ron Paul commented that there were only a "total of about eight or ten sentences" of "bad stuff" in the newsletters that he regularly used to publish under his name.[22] Therefore, in light of Paul's continuing evasions about the newsletters and with the hope of clarifying the matter definitively, *The New Republic* made excerpts of the letters available for all to see. The excerpts clearly indicated that Ron Paul was very much involved and aware of what was published in his newsletters. Here are a few other examples:

A December 1989 newsletter quoted by James Kirchick in the New Republic predicted "Racial Violence Will Fill Our Cities" because "mostly black welfare recipients will feel justified in stealing from mostly white 'haves.'"[23]

Another letter said "I think we can assume that 95 percent of the black men in that city [Washington] are semi-criminal or entirely criminal."[24]

An August 1992 edition of the Ron Paul Report labeled former Rep. Barbara Jordan (D) of Texas "the archetypal half-educated victimologist," according to the Houston Chronicle.[25]

Of course, Ron Paul is a Tea Partier who was quickly eliminated from the presidential race.

Third, we have the billionaire Koch brothers, David H. and Charles Koch. Behind every man-made, colossal, rapid, and robust organization, there has to be a major source of financial support. A list of the eight most powerful and politically influential businessmen published by ABC News puts the Koch brothers at numbers one and two. The article "Top 8 Most Powerful Businessmen Influencing Politics" by David Besnainou explained, "The rich have ideological beliefs just like other Americans. But their fortunes afford them an oversized influence in the political process. Once they acquire their billions, these heavy hitters tend to focus on changing the U.S. political climate and influencing global issues, either by using their clout to steer policy debates or using their money to back parties and candidates. The Koch Brothers are typically secretive and reluctant to speak in public...According to one estimate, they've contributed more than $100 million to conservative political causes, and a foundation that they back has trained thousands of Tea Party activists."[26]

There are several websites that claim to be the home or the official website of the Tea Party movement. In fact, I found it a bit confusing to determine which website was originally developed with the movement. There is www.TeaPartyPatriots.ning.com, www.TeaParty.org, and www.TeaPartyexpress.org, just to name a few. If you were to examine the "about" sections of their websites, you would find many similarities but different overall mission statements. TeaPartyPatriots.ning.com reads as follows:

Mission Statement

Our mission is to attract, educate, organize, and mobilize our fellow St. Louis area conservatives to secure a culture consistent with our three core values of Free Market Economics, Constitutionally Limited Government and Fiscal Responsibility.

Core Values
Proposed Language for Mission Statement
Core Principles of the Gateway Grassroots Initiative:

1. **Free Market Economics**. A free market is the economic

87

consequence of personal liberty. The founders believed that personal and economic freedom were indivisible, as do we. As government can do nothing but *distort the free expression of personal and economic liberty*, we therefore support limited government.

2. **Constitutionally Limited Government**. We, members of the Gateway Grassroots Initiative, are inspired by our founding documents and regard the Constitution of the United States as the supreme law of the land. We believe it is possible to know the original intent of the government our founders set forth and stand in support of that intent, as enumerated in such documents as, the Declaration of Independence and Federalist Papers. Like the founders, we are federalists, and support states rights for those powers not expressly stated in the Constitution. As the government is of the people, by the people and for the people, in all other matters we support the personal liberty of the individual, within the rule of law.

3. **Fiscal Responsibility**. A constitutionally limited government, designed to protect the blessings of liberty must be fiscally responsible or it will place *onerous burdens of taxation upon its citizenry, which unjustly restricts the very liberty* it is designed to protect and abrogates the rights it is designed to secure.

- **Fiscal Responsibility**
- **Constitutionally Limited Government**
- **Free Markets**

Fiscal Responsibility: Fiscal Responsibility by government honors and respects the freedom of the individual to spend the money that is the fruit of his or her own labor. A constitutionally limited government, designed to protect the blessings of liberty, must be fiscally responsible or it must subject its citizenry to high levels of taxation that unjustly restrict the liberty our Constitution was designed to protect. The runaway deficit spending as we now see in Washington D.C. *compels us to take action* because we know that a heavy

The Ugly Mouths of America!

burden of national debt is a *grave threat* to our national sovereignty and the personal and economic liberty of future generations.

Constitutionally Limited Government: We, the members of Gateway Grassroots, are inspired by our founding documents and regard the Constitution of the United States to be the supreme law of the land. We believe that it is possible to know the original intent of the government our founders set forth, and stand in support of that intent. Like the founders, we support states' rights for those powers not expressly stated in the Constitution. As the government is of the people, by the people and for the people, in all other matters we support the personal liberty of the individual, within the rule of law.

Free Markets: A free market is the economic consequence of personal liberty. The founders believed that personal and economic freedom were indivisible, as do we. Our current government's interference *distorts the free market and inhibits the pursuit of individual and economic liberty*. Therefore, we support a return to the free market principles on which this nation was founded and oppose government intervention into the operations of private business.[27] (emphasis mine)

TeaParty.org's "about" section reads as follows:

The Tea Party is a grassroots movement that calls awareness to any issue that challenges the security, sovereignty, or domestic tranquility of our beloved nation, the United States of America. From our founding, *the Tea Party represents the voice of the true owners of the United States:* WE THE PEOPLE.

Many are credited to be the founders of this movement; however, it was the brave souls of the men and women in 1773, known today as the Boston Tea Party, who dared to defy the greatest military might on earth. We are the beneficiaries of their courage.

The Tea Party includes those who possess a strong belief in the foundational Judeo-Christian values embedded in our great founding documents. We believe that the responsibility of our beloved nation is *entrenched within the hearts of true American Patriots* from every race, religion, national origin, and walk of life who share a common belief in the values which made and keep our beloved nation great. This belief led to the creation of the modern-day Tea Party. Many Republicans, Democrats, Libertarians, and Independents alike identify with the premises set forth by the Tea Party Movement, which is striking a chord and ringing true with the American Spirit.

We stand by the Constitution as inherently conservative. We serve as a beacon to the masses that have lost their way, a light illuminating the path to the original intentions of our Founding Fathers. We must raise a choir of voices declaring that America must stand on the values that made us great. Only then will the politically blind see and deaf hear!

By joining the Tea Party, you are taking a stand for our nation. You will be upholding the grand principles set forth in the U.S. Constitution and Bill of Rights.[28] (emphasis mine)

It then goes on to list fifteen nonnegotiable core beliefs. They are as follows:

1. Illegal aliens are here illegally.
2. Pro-domestic employment is indispensable.
3. A strong military is essential.
4. *Special interests must be eliminated.*
5. *Gun ownership is sacred.*
6. Government must be downsized.
7. The national budget must be balanced.
8. Deficit spending must end.
9. *Bailout and stimulus plans are illegal.*
10. Reducing personal income taxes is a must.
11. *Reducing business income taxes is mandatory.*
12. Political offices must be available to average citizens.
13. *Intrusive government must be stopped.*
14. English as our core language is required.

90

15. Traditional family values are encouraged.[29] (emphasis mine)

TeaPartyexpress.org has the following mission statement:

The Tea Party Express is proud to stand for six simple principles:

Propelled by millions of Tea Party supporters across the country, the Tea Party Express has become the most aggressive and influential national Tea Party group in the political arena. We are committed to identifying and supporting conservative candidates and causes that will champion tea party values and return our country to the Constitutional principles that have made America the "shining city on a hill."

No more bailouts
Reduce the size and intrusiveness of government
Stop raising our taxes
Repeal Obamacare
Cease out-of-control spending
Bring back American prosperity.[30] (emphasis mine)

On the surface this all sounds well and good, extremely patriotic, and supportive of the United States as the sovereign nation that has dominated the present-day civilized world of mankind. The wording used by these organizations can make one feel pride to be an American citizen; this, too, is good. But what else do their messages suggest? What questions do they raise?

The common thread found among Tea Partiers is a cry for smaller government. In fact, some of the statements made by the Tea Party border closely on making the current government administration an enemy of the movement, so it may be viewed by some as antigovernment. Let's go back and look at the phrases I have highlighted throughout the mission statements and make a few observations about what is really being said:

91

"distort the free expression of personal and economic liberty" – The word *distort* means *to misrepresent, falsify, or twist*. Here, then, the Tea Party activists are suggesting the government disrupts personal and economic liberty.

"onerous burdens of taxation upon its citizenry, which unjustly restricts the very liberty" – This tells us that the government strenuously and wearisomely places unjust burdens of tax on its citizens and restricts their freedom.

"the Tea Party represents the voice of the true owners of the United States" – I found this statement to be very interesting. The Tea Party is a small, mostly white organization, but by no means do they represent the voice of all of America; history tells us the Native Americans were here first, and millions of present-day Americans do not belong to the Tea Party.

"entrenched within the hearts of true American Patriots" – Does one, I wonder, have to be a Tea Party member to be an American Patriot?

And finally, there is this, which reveals the Tea Party's main target: "With conservatives in control of the House and poised to take over the Senate in 2012, the Tea Party Express has targeted President Barack Obama for defeat."

So there we have it: the Tea Party's main objective is to defeat Barack Obama and repeal his administration's governmental actions. One may ask, "Why is the president of the United States the enemy?"

Like the outspoken UMAs, the Tea Party movement is deeply rooted in the emotional grasp of patriotism. Based on the spreading of propaganda regarding the president, such as "he wasn't born in the US", "he's a Marxist", "he's a Communist", "he's a Muslim", or "he's anti-American" etc., it appears as if they have come to believe all that is put before them. Like sheep without a shepherd, yet having no clear leadership, they are told what to do, when to do it, and they do it.

92

Stuart Whatley a managing blog editor for the *Huffington Post* wrote regarding the Tea Party:

In *Authoritarianism & Polarization in American Politics*, a revealing work of political science published last year that unfortunately went somewhat unnoticed, Marc J. Hetherington and Jonathan D. Weiler describe a specific worldview -- *authoritarianism* -- which they argue lies at the heart of political polarization in modern American politics.

According to Hetherington and Weiler, authoritarians tend to rely more on emotion and instinct in decision-making, view politics in black and white, resent confusion or ambiguity in the social order, and are suspicious of specific groups who they believe could alter that order (typically gays and immigrants)...

Most every characteristic of an authoritarian worldview lends itself well to the impassioned rhetoric of the Tea Party movement and to the shrewd players operating behind the scenes and atop the soap box. The movement's overly simplified, often-confused solutions to complex problems align with authoritarians' Manichean worldview...

The Tea Party presents a series of demands that have little to do with the interests of its members who are the common everyday workers. For example, they cry out for a downsized government with fewer regulations, lower taxes for the upper class and big corporations, and cutbacks to social programs like education, Medicare, and Medicaid. These best serve the interests of the upper class and big corporations, but it does very little for the average Americans living from pay check to pay check, or for those previous hard-working seniors who have now retired and may need medical assistance. Stuart Whatley continues in his article by describing very basic core problems confronting the Tea party.

At its core, the Tea Party movement is rife with contradiction, incoherence and a willful contempt for facts or reason. It is but a parody of the legitimate movements for which American democracy has historically been held in such high

93

regard. It is, in fact, the latest installment in quite another American tradition: the exploitation of frustrated, desperate, and susceptible people by monied interests and profiteers.

The impetus for the Civil Rights movement was centuries of racially based oppression at all levels of American government and society. The logic behind its call for equality was overwhelming. Now consider the Tea Party movement, whose foremost demand of a president who in his first month passed one of the biggest tax cuts ever...is for tax cuts. The movement's incoherence is only illuminated further when this demand is uttered in the same sentence as its call for deficit reduction.

Though the movement claims to have no defined leadership, there are public figures and entities who nevertheless carry that mantle, which has led to perhaps its greatest irony: a portion of the American populace who carries a populist banner against the coddling of greedy bankers is led by some of the country's most cynical and base profiteers.[31]

Following the profiteers of the Tea Party leads us to the Koch brothers. Any mobster, gangster, or organized criminal must appear good, considerate, thoughtful, and even full of kindness in the eyes of the populace. The deceptive smoky mirror is a useful tool that serves to veil the objectives of their actions. In addition, it binds in loyalty the beneficiaries, who themselves are often greedy for power and money. The mobsters of old were known for their smooching with politicians, big business, and religion. The Koch brothers are not much different. The only change is that we are now a global community. Organized crimes have now reached global proportions, with multimillionaire and billionaire criminals effectively influencing international business, the political arena, and religion. It is as the Bible reads at 2 Corinthians 11:14: "And no wonder, Satan himself keeps transforming himself into an angel of light."

David Hamilton Koch is a well-known American businessman, philanthropist, and political activist. Together, he and his brother Charles Koch own and operate Koch

The Ugly Mouths of America!

Industries, the second-largest privately held company in the United States.[32] Headquartered in Wichita, Kansas, Koch Industries has annual revenues of an estimated one hundred billion dollars. The company owns oil refineries in Alaska, Texas, and Minnesota and controls four thousand miles of pipeline. In addition, Koch Industries owns a diverse group of companies, including Georgia-Pacific, Stainmaster Carpet, and Invista (makers of spandex and polyester, among other products). David and his brother Charles have a combined net worth of nearly thirty-five billion dollars. Together, they have donated millions of dollars to charities and have established and founded their own charitable organizations.

Interestingly, Greenpeace issued a report in 2008 identifying Koch Industries as a "kingpin of climate science denial." According to *The New Yorker*, the report showed that, from 2005 to 2008, the Koches vastly outdid Exxon Mobil in giving money to organizations fighting legislation related to climate change; they underwrote a huge network of foundations, think tanks, and political front groups. Indeed, the brothers have funded opposition campaigns against so many Obama administrative policies—from health care reform to the economic stimulus program—that, in political circles, their ideological network is known as the Kochtopus.[33] The University of Massachusetts at Amherst's Political Economy Research Institute named Koch Industries one of the top ten air polluters in the United States.[34]

A popular organization promoted by "the great American" Sean Hannity and that is also funded by the deceptive Koch brothers is the Heritage Foundation. The Heritage Foundation is an environmental skepticism organization which has argued against human involvement in global warming. *The New Yorker* article "Covert Operations" by Jane Mayer reads,

In a 2002 memo, the Republican political consultant Frank Luntz wrote that so long as "voters believe there is no consensus about global warming within the scientific community" the status quo would prevail. The key for opponents of environmental reform, he said, was to question

95

the science—a public-relations strategy that the tobacco industry used effectively for years to forestall regulation. The Kochs have funded many sources of environmental skepticism, such as the Heritage Foundation, which has argued that "scientific facts gathered in the past 10 years do not support the notion of catastrophic human-made warming." The brothers have given money to more obscure groups, too, such as the Independent Women's Forum, which opposes the presentation of global warming as a scientific fact in American public schools. Until 2008, the group was run by Nancy Pfotenhauer, a former lobbyist for Koch Industries. Mary Beth Jarvis, a vice-president of a Koch subsidiary, is on the group's board.[35]

The Kochtopus network is deeply rooted in organizations that are in opposition to President Obama and his administration's laws and policies. Among the many organizations that were founded by David and Charles Koch is Americans for Prosperity. The article "Covert Operations" continues:

,Americans for Prosperity has worked closely with the Tea Party since the movement's inception. In the weeks before the first Tax Day protests, in April, 2009, Americans for Prosperity hosted a Web site offering supporters "Tea Party Talking Points." The Arizona branch urged people to send tea bags to Obama; the Missouri branch urged members to sign up for "Taxpayer Tea Party Registration" and provided directions to nine protests. The group continues to stoke the rebellion. The North Carolina branch recently launched a "Tea Party Finder" Web site, advertised as "a hub for all the Tea Parties in North Carolina."

The anti-government fervor infusing the 2010 elections represents a political triumph for the Kochs. By giving money to "educate," fund, and organize Tea Party protesters, they have helped turn their private agenda into a mass movement.[36]

The Tea Party claims to be a "grassroots" movement. This term implies that its formation, drive of the movement,

96

as well as it support is all natural and spontaneous. This is far different from a movement that is orchestrated by traditional power structures. However, the Tea Party is more of an 'artificial turf' movement, its members like to use the term, "grassroots", but it's formed, orchestrated, and supported by big business profiteers. The Tea Party elite business personnel have used the emergence and influence of the Tea Party to quietly gain more control and to channel their political agenda.

That same article continued,

The Republican campaign consultant said of the family's political activities, "To call them under the radar is an understatement. They are underground!" Another former Koch adviser said, "They're smart. This right-wing, redneck stuff works for them. They see this as a way to get things done without getting dirty themselves." Rob Stein, a Democratic political strategist who has studied the conservative movement's finances, said that the Kochs are "at the epicenter of the anti-Obama movement. But it's not just about Obama. They would have done the same to Hillary Clinton. They did the same with Bill Clinton. They are out to destroy progressivism."[37]

It is one thing to be in opposition to an organization or a movement, but Koch Industries has dirty, secretive dealings that go deeper: it has violated United States federal laws.

In May 2008, Koch Industries sent a newly hired compliance and ethics manager, Ms. Ludmilla Egorova-Farines, to investigate the management of a subsidiary in southern France. After just a week of investigation, she discovered that the company had paid bribes to win contracts. By September of that year, clear evidence indicated improper payments dating back to 2002 that had been authorized by the business director and used to secure contracts in six countries.

"Those activities constitute violations of criminal law," Koch Industries wrote in a December 8, 2008, letter giving details of its findings. The letter was made public in a civil court ruling in France in September 2010; the document had never before been reported by the media.[38]

Instead of rewarding Ms. Egorova-Farines, she was removed from the investigation and later terminated in June 2009.

In addition, a *Bloomberg Markets* investigation found that Koch industries used improper payments to win business contracts in Africa, India, and the Middle East, including selling millions of dollars of petrochemical equipment to Iran. This act violated the governmental sanctions that were in place against Iran due to its involvement in sponsoring global terrorism.[39]

In 1999, a Texas jury imposed a charge of $296 million on Koch Industries. The guilty verdict was for negligence that resulted in the death of two teenagers due to a leaky underground butane pipeline. At the time, this was the largest compensatory damages won in a judgment of a wrongful death case against a corporation in US history.[40]

From 1999 to 2003, Koch Industries was assessed more than $400 million in fines, penalties, and judgments.[41]

In December 1999, a civil jury found that Koch Industries had taken oil it didn't pay for from federal land by inaccurately measuring the amount of crude oil it extracted. Koch Industries paid a $25 million settlement to the United States.[42]

If you were to really research the Koch operations, you would find enough crooked and twisted secretive dealings to compose an entire manuscript. *The New Yorker* article "Covert Operations: put it this way: "The Kochs continued to disperse their money, creating slippery organizations with generic-sounding names, and this made it difficult to ascertain the extent of their influence in Washington. In 1990, *Citizens for a Sound Economy* created

The Ugly Mouths of America!

a spinoff group, *Citizens for the Environment*, which called acid rain and other environmental problems 'myths.' When the Pittsburgh *Post-Gazette* investigated the matter, it discovered that the spinoff group had 'no citizen membership of its own.'"[43]

Many of us may not have known or perhaps we may not remember that David Koch once ran for public office in 1980. As a supporter of the Libertarian Party, the Koch brothers were backing Ed Clark, who ran against Ronald Regan. David was placed on the ticket in the Vice-Presidential slot. The ticket's slogan was "The Libertarian Party has only one source of funds: You."[44] *The New Yorker* article "Covert Operations" relates the party's agenda:

Many of the ideas propounded in the 1980 campaign presaged the Tea Party movement. Ed Clark told The Nation that libertarians were getting ready to stage "a very big tea party," because people were "sick to death" of taxes. The Libertarian Party platform called for the abolition of the F.B.I. and the C.I.A., as well as of federal regulatory agencies, such as the Securities and Exchange Commission and the Department of Energy. The Party wanted to end Social Security, minimum-wage laws, gun control, and all personal and corporate income taxes; it proposed the legalization of prostitution, recreational drugs, and suicide. Government should be reduced to only one function: the protection of individual rights. William F. Buckley, Jr., a more traditional conservative, called the movement "Anarcho-Totalitarianism."[45]

Although David Koch did not win his seat in the political arena, the Koch brothers were not deterred from their hard-lined libertarian political agenda for America. Making use of their humongous financial resources, they have strategically given millions of dollars to political campaigns, advocacy groups, and lobbyist. *The New Yorker* article "Covert Operations" explains:

Charles Koch seems to have approached both business and politics with the deliberation of an engineer. "To bring about

99

social change," he told Doherty, requires "a strategy" that is "vertically and horizontally integrated," spanning "from idea creation to policy development to education to grassroots organizations to lobbying to litigation to political action." The project, he admitted, was extremely ambitious. "We have a radical philosophy," he said.[46]

It is the Koch brothers who have delivered falsified propaganda to the general American public, painting a negative image of our government and our current president. They want us to believe and have successfully promoted the idea that President Obama is a socialist and an elitist with a radical agenda who has no interest in the building of a united, powerful nation under the principles of liberty, justice, and freedom for all. To a large extent, they have made the president of the United States and his administration out to be an enemy of the free world. Their message also sounds a lot like the resounding voices of the UMAs.

Chapter 6: A House Divided

For those of us who are Bible readers and perhaps consider ourselves Christians, we may be familiar with the words recorded in Mark 3:24–26. There the Lord, Christ Jesus, makes a profound statement that has proven to be very true throughout all of history. If you read the surrounding context of the scripture, you will find that Christ's reason for saying it was because he was again defending his teachings. His accusers are the scribes, the Jewish religious leaders of his day who have come down from Jerusalem. These scribes are saying that "[Christ] has Beelzebub [the ruler of the demons, Satan] and he expels the demons by means of the ruler of the demons." Christ then calls his followers to him and begins to teach them by means of an illustration. Jesus says, "How can Satan expel Satan? Why if a kingdom [or government] becomes divided against itself, that kingdom cannot stand. And if a house becomes divided against itself, that house will not be able to stand. Also, if Satan has risen up against himself and become divided, he cannot stand, but is coming to an end."

In our government there is more division among the political houses than ever before. In fact, America, although a great nation, has become exceedingly divided. There is no longer a proper balance between the Republicans and the Democrats, the far left and the far right, Christians and non-Christians, believers and atheists, natural-born citizens and immigrants, or unions and nonunion organizations. Our society, with its many different cultures and the different beliefs that follow from that, has become divided on the basis of freedom and liberty, with each one of us feeling we have the exclusive right to express ourselves and live our lives through our own perception of right and wrong. On the surface this may appear right or good for society. But the harsh reality is that it causes many laws to be passed that may seem ridiculous to others, criminals to get away with the most horrendous crimes, and the innocent to be found guilty or to be treated as such.

An example of a law that was passed to protect our citizens, but was challenged due to different beliefs of freedom and religion, can be demonstrated in the following experience: Shortly after the devastating bombing on 9/11 and George W. Bush's announcement of the war on terrorism, US security forces started to beef up security measures throughout the country. In 2001, a Muslim woman had obtained a driver's license issued by Florida State with a photo in which her face was completely veiled. The only part of her face visible in the photo, through a small slit in the hooded covering, was her eyes. Due to the new security measures and laws, the state demanded that the woman retake the photo, but she refused. As a result, the state revoked her driver's license. The woman, feeling she was now a victim, filed a lawsuit against the state, saying "I don't show my face to strangers or unrelated males".[1]

On the surface this may seem like a ridiculous situation. How could anyone have a state-issued identification card that does not show the features of her face in order to be identified? To put it humorously, it could be likened to taking a photo of a person's rear end or backside and using it as his or her photo ID.

Her case was taken up by the American Civil Liberties Union (ACLU), which saw the case as a test of religious freedom. Randall Marshall, Legal Director of the ACLU of Florida was quoted as saying, "We live in a religiously diverse country where everyone is supposed to have the right to practice and worship as they choose... Yet, here we have a case where the government is questioning one woman's sincerely held religious beliefs and then forcing her to compromise them under the false pretext of national security."[2] Conservative commentators ridiculed the case, saying it would be absurd to allow people to obscure their faces in ID photos. However, at that time, there were fourteen states where a driver's license could be obtained without a photo having to be taken. I personally thought it was beyond reason, even idiotic, to have a person take an identification photo in which his or her face could not be viewed—that defeats the purpose of the photo. At taxpayers' expense, the case went to trial. After three days of

102

testimony, Circuit Judge Janet C. Thorpe ruled that the free exercise of religion would not be infringed on by having her show her face on her license, thus agreeing with state authorities that the practice could help terrorists conceal their identities.

A second example of division of liberty or privileges is found in the fight over illegal immigration laws. Every functional organization has to be governed by rules or laws to establish a measure of order; otherwise, there would be chaos. Even the true God, who gave man freedom and the right to choose, saw the need to give laws and governing principals to his free people (Genesis 2:16–17). This is also true of man-made nations, authorities, and governments.

Illegal immigration can be defined as the migration of foreign citizens into a country under circumstances in which such people do not meet the legal requirements for entering that country, that is, when they are violating the immigration laws of that jurisdiction. Under Title 8 Section 1325 of the United States Code, "Improper Entry by Alien," it clearly states that any citizen of any country other than the United States who enters the country illegally has committed a crime.[3]

Again, I must note that the factor of imbalance is a very prevalent and dominating force in our current system of things. There are some states and organizations that go to the extreme in fighting illegal immigration, and then there are some who appear to want to ignore or not recognize the ongoing problem at all, choosing not even to utter the words "illegal aliens" (instead they refer to them as "undocumented immigrants").

There is nothing wrong with saying "undocumented immigrants," but it does sound softer and seems to lessen the impact of committing a federal crime. It's almost as if the term *illegal immigrant* is bad or has become politically incorrect. The National Association of Hispanic Journalists (NAHJ) had this to say about the term on September 16, 2010:

The National Association of Hispanic Journalists (NAHJ) calls on our nation's news media to use accurate terminology in its coverage of immigration and to stop dehumanizing undocumented immigrants...

NAHJ is concerned with the increasing use of pejorative terms to describe the estimated 11 million undocumented people living in the United States. NAHJ is particularly troubled with the growing trend of the news media to use the word 'illegals' as a noun, shorthand for 'illegal aliens.'

Using the word in this way is grammatically incorrect and crosses the line by criminalizing the person, not the action they are purported to have committed. NAHJ calls on the media to never use 'illegals' in headlines... [and] to avoid 'Illegal alien.' Alternative terms are 'undocumented worker,' or 'undocumented immigrant.[4]

Based on this explanation the NAHJ provides they suggest the terms 'illegals' or 'illegal alien' is grammatically incorrect and dehumanize the person or deprives him or her of individuality.

The American Civil Liberties Union, the same union that defended the woman with the veil, says this on their website: "No human being is illegal. The Constitution guarantees the fundamental rights and civil liberties of every person in this country. Upholding the rights of the politically disenfranchised is vital; when the government has the power to deny legal rights and due process to one group of people; it puts all our rights in danger."[5]

So the defining of illegal alien or undocumented immigrant becomes more complex. It should be apparent that if someone enters the country without the proper legal documents he or she becomes illegal. Therefore it should be apparent, that as an adult, when you knowingly and purposefully do something illegal to the extent of the action it is a violation or a crime. Contrary to the ACLU statement, the Constitution of the United States was thus referring to those who legally are applying the laws of the land. Here is a case of making the logical become illogical and more complex.

Since Barack Obama became president, I have observed more fighting between the two political parties in the media than ever before. The intermingling of the conservative movement and its Tea Partiers as well as the labor unions has furthermore caused the situation to worsen. The sad thing is that all of this is at the expense of the American people. We are the ones who really suffer the most from the ongoing bickering. It appears that the interests of the American people are no longer the main concern of the government; instead, the interests of the individual politician, the political party, and the special interest group receive the most attention. It isn't just on a political level that this division is occurring, however. It is evident between cultures, societies, religions, races, and ethnic backgrounds.

You may recall that in the introduction I mentioned I did not vote for Obama or anyone else in the 2008 election. I explained my reasoning as being that I did not know much about Obama and that I am for the most part neutral toward the politics of this world. Let me expound on this position of neutrality.

According to the *Oxford English Dictionary*, neutrality is defined as "not supporting either side in a conflict; without distinctive or positive characteristics", it does not mean that you have no opinion. So, when it comes to supporting one political party or representative of that party over another, in this case, your vote, I am neutral. But then the question is: why neutrality?

First, I understand and agree that every citizen of legal voting age who has registered to vote has the right to vote. Also, I recognize and appreciate that our forefathers took on great obstacles to guarantee us that right. But I understand voting to be a *right* and not a command or obligation. Some say that voting is "your obligation and the American thing to do" or part of "the American way of life." On the contrary, our country is America, and the American way of life is to be governed by our political system. One is

105

not obligated to participate in voting, but rather obligated not to oppose the governmental system.

Being neutral does not indicate that one doesn't support the laws or pay their taxes. Neither does neutrality mean showing or having any disrespect for the representatives of any political party. In fact, true neutrality means having much more respect for people than the UMAs, from what I have observed. The simple and clear principle of proper respect can be discerned from the words recorded in the Bible at Romans 13:1. The apostle Paul is discussing having proper respect for the ruling authorities: "Let every soul be in subjection to the superior authorities, for there is no authority, except by God. The existing authorities stand placed in their *relative* position by God. Therefore, he who opposes the authority has taken a stand against the arrangement of God..." (emphasis mine). Verse 7 continues, "Render to all their dues, for him who calls for the tax, the tax; for him who calls for the tribute, the tribute, for him who calls for fear, such fear; for him who calls for honor, such honor."

A "relative position" refers simply to a subordinate position in relation to God's authority. What this means is that God has allowed these politicians and political organizations to exist and to exercise a measure of authority, but it is the true God, our Grand Creator, who is the absolute authority.

Second, we greatly depend on the main stream media to report to us the news of the day. In view of politics and favorable ratings, the media has the ability to twist and turn any story so that it becomes popular. That being the case, how could anyone truly know what is true or false in order to know what side of an issue to stand on? We must trust our authorities and elected officials to handle governmental issues, make good decisions, and inform us as to the unbiased truth. In most cases, I would say this trust has diminished.

In the wake of 9/11, terrorism, the current wars, and nuclear, chemical, and biological threats, we can easily see the need for global peace. However, one may ask whether the divisive politics of this world are capable of bringing about true and lasting peace on a global scale. In view of our past and current condition, the answer to that question is a resounding no.

It is sad to say, but when you discuss politics with a stranger, a friend, or anyone at all, often you will hear that you have "a choice of the lesser of two evils." I do not necessarily agree with this line of thinking; however, I do believe that when you have a good man or woman who is running for office, they have to work with and through a political system that is filled with corruption, greed, and power. Therefore, it is very difficult for a person with good intentions to accomplish his or her objectives without compromising any principles or offending others.

If you were to do research on the first-century Christians, the followers of Christ, you will find that they did not get involved in the political arena. In fact, it was the Sadducees, the Pharisees, and the Sanhedrin who mingled with the Roman political leaders of Jesus's day. Jesus and his disciples remained separate. It was the Sanhedrin that was looking for false witnesses to condemn Christ. It was the governor, Pontius Pilate, who held Christ on trial for his life. The apostles and his disciples were not involved in politics. Christ said of his true followers in prayer, "they are no part of the world, just as he was not part of the world" (John 17:16).

As a Christian, I choose to remain neutral to political affairs. I observe what is going on around me in our society and the corrupt world of politics, war, and violence. I commend the good efforts and policies of many politicians and their parties. In fact I strongly commend them, realizing we need them to exist. However, it is my choice to remain separate from the world of politics. I have chosen to obey the laws of the land, pay owed taxes, follow the principles of the Bible, and to be educated with regard to my surroundings. I believe the principles of the Bible include keeping a neutral but very observant position.

The struggles of President Obama within our nation and among foreign nations are many indeed. They include health care reform, which the UMAs like to refer to as "Obamacare"; the subprime mortgage crisis; the US deficit; unemployment; the withdrawal of our troops in Iran, the buildup of our troops in Afghanistan, and the support of our forces in Libya; the future of social security, Medicaid, and Medicare; the raising of the debt ceiling; and the increasing price of oil, among many other problems he's faced in just his first three years. Yet the bickering continues for months and years, so that nothing or very little really gets accomplished. This paralyzes our society.

But one may wonder: why so much division? A major factor that contributes to division is public opinion. Influencing public opinion is mainly control exerted by the public media forces. These are the sources of what the public hears, sees, and eventually believes as happening within our country and around the world. We must remember that in the 1930s and early 1940s, there was no Internet access or computers and in most cases televisions in people's households, but only a radio to listen to or a newspaper to read. People trusted their governmental officials and their religious leaders in the pulpits, and overall they had more respect for authority. When an ugly mouth would speak out in opposition to the mainstream media, he or she could easily be silenced. In fact, some of the things the UMAs express in our modern day and time would have caused them to be viewed as un- or anti-American in the past. For example, it was unheard-of to call the president of the United States "an idiot," "stupid," "racist," "a Marxist," "a Nazi," and so much more. Even if one had privately held those thoughts, views, or feelings toward the president, they were kept private, only being discussed at the dinner table among family or close associates. They were definitely never proclaimed by the public media.

Television proved early on to have a major influence on the way we thought, viewed ourselves, and developed our opinions of others. Due to its global reach, it also served to encourage the freewheeling American lifestyle and culture in foreign nations. The TV programs of the fifties and sixties

108

featured simple, clean lifestyles that were viewed daily by the American public. These classics examples include *I Love Lucy, The Andy Griffith Show, The Dick Van Dyke Show, My Three Sons, Green Acres, The Beverly Hillbillies,* and *Petticoat Junction.* There wasn't any cursing or sex or any form of filth presented on these programs. People enjoyed the clean humor, the simple lifestyles; for the most part, those of us outside the shows were also moral, humane, and decent. Of course, there are exceptions to every scenario. In the fifties and sixties we had our share of hippies, gangs, and drug users, but their conduct was not generally viewed as the norm or as a positive influence on television. The more controversial shows, such as soap operas and late-night talk programs, came on television when children were normally in school or late at night when children were normally in bed. At that time, the daily news programs came on primarily at specific times of the day, like in the early morning, in the evening around five or six, or late at night around ten. Adults could easily monitor what their children were viewing.

In the 1950s, Americans watched the daily news on four major television networks: ABC, CBS, NBC, and Dumont. This news opened the eyes of American viewers to what was happening in the other countries and more saliently, what effects our actions were having around the world. As the popularity of television grew at an astonishingly rapid pace, so did radio's popularity, especially as listeners would listen to it while driving back and forth from work. Daily news reports quickly became propaganda for public opinion.

The article, "Selling a New Vision of America to the World", by Al Yarrow helps us to understand the necessity of American propaganda both domestically and abroad in the 1950's. America had experienced two World Wars, engaged the Korean War from 1950-1953, and confronted the Cold War with the USSR. The country needed to believe in American values and its government. The world needed to see America as a land of opportunities. The article explains:

The main propaganda battlefield of the late 1940s and early 1950s was in Europe, as the United States sought to ensure

The Ugly Mouths of America!

that Western Europe would remain non-Communist and the Soviet Union tried to exploit and fan anti-Americanism. By the mid-1950s, however, the main front for propaganda was the Communist world itself and the nonaligned countries of the Third World.

Yet foreign policy was not the only context for changes in propaganda messages. Domestic concerns and messages disseminated by politicians, media, business leaders, educators, and others for domestic consumption also framed what information and ideas about the United States were disseminated to the world. These opinion leaders spoke of a "new era" of "people's capitalism," or a "changed America" that had conquered the business cycle, producing a country in which "everybody's rich." The idea that a new chapter of American history (and of the history of capitalism) had dawned was a frequent subject of news reports, political speeches, business communications, and even elementary and secondary school curricula, particularly after the Korean War.[6]

America's favorite pastimes became more popular with television's growth. Popular with the man of the house were sports such as baseball, football, and eventually basketball that eased our minds of the realities, stress, and concerns of world events. Soap operas and game shows, such as *The Price is Right*, *The Dating Game*, and *Let's Make a Deal* were more popular among women viewers throughout the week. However, with popularity comes power. As advertising companies increased their profits, politicians, unionized organizations, religious groups, and others saw the benefit of taking advantage of the media forces. They quickly discovered that people could be easily swayed in their thinking and feelings by the use of successful advertising campaigns and society-enhanced promotional television programs.

The television audience would see an explosion of designer clothing, extravagant places to visit, luxury homes with unique furniture, expensive cars, and more, all which enhanced the America vision of success. As the 1960s concluded, we viewed more advertisements that opposed

110

negative society trends that were less popular or frowned upon, such as smoking, use of drugs and other unwholesome activities.

During the 1960s, controversial issues of the day in politics, religion, and society were depicted on television and discussed on talk radio. In fact, television had become the main source for news and politics. For example, coverage of the Vietnam War—the first televised war—"brought the 'horror of war' night after night into people's living rooms and eventually inspired revulsion and exhaustion."[7] Negative coverage of the war was very instrumental in swaying some Americans to have negative opinions toward the war and, perhaps surprisingly, also toward its veterans.

Critical views of the war also led to antiwar demonstrations by religious organizations, civil rights activists, labor unions, college students, governmental institutions, and other groups. Many of these organizations were often in disagreement on many other current issues but were all united in their opposition to the Vietnam War. This opposition, along with the civil rights movement of the 1960s, proved to be one of the most divisive forces in American history.

The civil rights campaigns resulted from the mistreatment of black Americans for decades. The first major accomplishment of the movement was in 1954, when a unanimous decision was made by the Supreme Court that segregation in public schools was unconstitutional and that black students could attend originally segregated white schools. This ruling proved to be a major victory for the National Association for the Advancement of Color People (NAACP), which had been founded in 1909. Although this ruling was accepted by the majority of Americans, there were many who opposed and feared whites and blacks attending schools in unity.

A second watershed moment in the fight against racial discrimination and segregation occurred in 1955, when Mrs. Rosa Parks refused to give up her seat to make room for a white passenger on a bus at the demand of the white

111

bus driver. Her act of defiance caused her much hardship, including her arrest, and resulted in her losing her job as a seamstress at a local department store. This quiet, courageous stand taken by Mrs. Parks proved eventually to be an important moment in history that helped change America.

The challenge to end discrimination and segregation has been an ongoing battle in America ever since slavery has been outlawed and our borders opened. Not only is there racial discrimination between the whites and the blacks, but in a society with many different ethical backgrounds and cultures, there is the continuing problem of discrimination and segregation against Hispanics, Latinos, Asians, Indians, Jews, Muslims, Christians, Atheists, and others.

With the advancement of technology and telecommunication, the divisive forces that challenge our society have become more visible. From the 1970s onward, television and radio, which have now become digital and satellite, as well as, eventually, the World Wide Web have proven to be major influences on our individual opinions. Politicians, unions, lobbyists, big businesses, Wall Street, and religious and other organizations have taken full advantage of these powerful resources. Today, billions of dollars are spent each year on advertising simply because of its power for influence on the mind. These powerful resources really work.

Barack Obama ran a very successful media-based campaign in 2007 that earned him the US presidency in 2008. He was the first major politician to make full use of social-network marketing, interactive campaigning, and sponsorship by means of digital media. According to *The Washington Post*, his 2008 presidential campaign raised over half a billion dollars online in just twenty-one months, thus ushering in a new digital era in presidential fundraising.[8]

Due to this compelling aggregate force of media resources, opportunist individuals, as well as political and nonpolitical organizations have been able to increase their

112

influence, propaganda, impact, and wealth on a much larger scale and a much larger playing field than ever before. As a result, a society of diverse dynamic influences flourished.

Today, politicians and the UMAs take full advantage of this power. Spreading both negative and often untrue and inaccurate reports, they form opinions that manipulate the American public. Organizations with huge financial resources use TARP moneys, payouts, and undisclosed agreements to push forward agendas that benefit them but often disregard public needs and concerns. The Ugly Mouths of America, too, are benefited in this way, by organizations and individuals who want to promote certain viewpoints to the public.

Rush Limbaugh, Sean Hannity, Glenn Beck, Neal Boortz, and other UMAs masters receive hefty sponsorship fees for their conservative radio talk programs and public events. Their sponsors pay for advertisements that often masquerade as patriotic and informative political news. Some of these sponsoring organizations are the Heritage Foundation and Americans for Prosperity (a Tea Party group founded by David Koch), as well as the latter's rival, Freedom Works. These organizations pay for promotional tie-ins and regular commercials in which the host UMA praises or defends the group's agenda. Michael Harrison, the founder and publisher of *Talkers Magazine*, was quoted as saying, "The point that people don't realize is that [the UMA radio personalities] are in the same business that people like Casey Kasem are in—and what they do is no different than from people who broadcast from used car lots or restaurants or endorse the local roofer or gardener."[9] The UMAs are unique only in that they have a way of blending this advertisement into their conversation so that it appears natural, politically correct, and patriotic.

Heritage Foundation Vice President of Operations and Marketing Genevieve Wood expressed it this way: "We approach it the way anyone approaches advertising: where is our audience that wants to buy what you sell?" He concludes that the UMAs' audience "fit that model for us. They promote conservative ideas and that's what we do."[10]

113

And they do this to the tune of many millions of dollars each year and with the consequence of making the captured audience think and feel the way they want it to think and feel. It becomes a very powerful, persuasive influence.

Shortly after President Obama won elected office in 2008, Rush Limbaugh went on record as hoping that Obama and his administration would be a complete failure. The following is a transcript from his radio broadcast on January 16, 2009:

I got a request here from a major American print publication. "Dear Rush: For the Obama [Immaculate] Inauguration we are asking a handful of very prominent politicians, statesmen, scholars, businessmen, commentators, and economists to write 400 words on their hope for the Obama presidency. We would love to include you. If you could send us 400 words on your hope for the Obama presidency, we need it by Monday night, that would be ideal." Now, we're caught in this trap again. The premise is, what is your "hope." My hope, and please understand me when I say this. I disagree fervently with the people on our side of the aisle who have caved and who say, "Well, I hope he succeeds. We've got to give him a chance." Why? They didn't give Bush a chance in 2000. Before he was inaugurated the search-and-destroy mission had begun. I'm not talking about search-and-destroy, but I've been listening to Barack Obama for a year-and-a-half. I know what his politics are. I know what his plans are, as he has stated them. I don't want them to succeed.

If I wanted Obama to succeed, I'd be happy the Republicans have laid down. And I would be encouraging Republicans to lay down and support him. Look, what he's talking about is the absorption of as much of the private sector by the US government as possible, from the banking business, to the mortgage industry, the automobile business, to health care. I do not want the government in charge of all of these things. I don't want this to work. So I'm thinking of replying to the guy, "Okay, I'll send you a response, but I don't need 400 words, I need four: I hope he fails." [interruption] What are you

114

laughing at? See, here's the point. Everybody thinks it's outrageous to say. Look, even my staff, "Oh, you can't do that." Why not? Why is it any different, what's new, what is unfair about my saying I hope liberalism fails? Liberalism is our problem. Liberalism is what's gotten us dangerously close to the precipice here. Why do I want more of it? I don't care what the Drive-By story is. I would be honored if the Drive-By Media headlined me all day long.[11]

Rush Limbaugh's friends Sean Hannity, Mark Levin, Glenn Beck, and Neal Boortz are an amalgamate force determined to spread only negative propaganda about President Obama and his administration. The Ugly Mouths' supporting cast—Fox News, the Tea Party Movement, the Heritage Foundation, Americans for Prosperity, and Freedom Works, all of which reach millions of Americans each day—have used a divide-and-conquer strategy to try to destroy support for the president and his administration in an effort to make it appear to be a failed presidency.

With the repeal of the Fairness Doctrine in 1987, the Ugly Mouths easily and successfully united. No longer did holders of broadcasting licenses have to present both sides of controversial issues to the American public in an honest, equitable, and balanced fashion; they could now twist and spin, tell half-truths, and more, presenting the so-called news any way they wanted. This fueled the growth of the modern-day Tea Party movement on which many Republicans now piggyback in order to succeed.

The stalemate preventing the success of Obama's presidency is not a result of people sharing meaningful different opinions. It is by design! The enemies of the Obama administration are within our government. They are Republicans, some Democrats, Tea Partiers, and extremely big businessmen, such as David and Charles Koch. They are organizations and individuals, such as the UMAs who are supported by masked "patriotic" charities that really have less interest in the prosperous development of our nation than in the growth of their own prosperity and power. Among them are those who have had the revelation that the election of an Afro-American into the highest office in the land is a

115

possible threat to corporate white America. Patrick J. Buchanan writes in the book *Suicide of a Superpower*, "Sensing their country slipping away and their abandonment by their own elites, middle and working class whites have turned to talk show hosts and television commentators, Rush Limbaugh and Glenn Beck, as well as Sarah Palin. But the demoralization is deep. Just nine months into Obama's presidency, a survey by the National Journal found that a plurality of white Americans over thirty not only had lost confidence in Wall Street and corporate America but in the U.S. Government."[12]

The November 2010 midterm elections proved to be the most expensive midterm elections in US history. Millions of dollars were contributed from outside special interest groups, with "you wash my back and I will eventually wash yours" mentality. Deals were made to gather momentum for so-called Tea Party Republicans, and the UMAs proudly broadcast their support for such candidates. As a result, there was a resurgence of the Republican Party, which had a huge win in the House of Representatives. In addition, many of the so-called Tea Party Republicans won over Democratic opponents when the time came to make policy decisions. This gave their conservative views a stronger voice in government. In addition, racial hatred has brought about a new and powerful stagnation that is holding our country hostage.

The unions and labor boards soon came into this scenario, showing their support for the Democrats who controlled the Senate. This resulted in more bickering, stalling, and confrontations that have caused American prosperity to snail, stop, and in some cases reverse. The threat of a double-dip recession continues to linger, and the economy has still not recovered. Until there is a uniting of forces and a balance restored among our leaders, we the American people and our nation as a whole will continue to suffer. Simply stated by the Lord, "...if a kingdom [or government] becomes divided against itself, that kingdom cannot stand. And if a house becomes divided against itself, that house will not be able to stand. Also, if Satan has risen up against himself and becomes divided he cannot stand,

116

but is coming to an end." Could it be that our way of governing is so divisive and ineffective that our political system and our country as we know it is now coming to its end?

Chapter 7: Obama's America

I remember when I first heard that Senator Barack Obama had announced his intention to run for the highest office in the land. I was standing in line at a local Walgreens store when a young Caucasian lady, most likely a college student, approached me and asked if I was going to support the senator in his run for the presidency. My first thought was that in a time when America was engaged in a war on terrorism and had a prime enemy named Saddam Hussein, a black man named Barack Hussein Obama could not possibly win the presidency. Second, I thought Mr. Obama was most likely a Muslim, and third, I thought I simply did not know anything about the man. My answer to the young college student was simple: "I'm really not interested in Barack Obama." After the passing of some time, however, like for the masses of so many others, Senator Obama drew out my interest. I was proud when I heard the man speak for the first time. His words were those of a man of great intelligence, and they reflected the education of an astute Harvard graduate. His appearance was that of a well-groomed, handsome, young African-American, and he was also a family man who had an equally intelligent, attractive, and educated wife. Due to his message of hope and change, coupled with his public appearance, Obama's popularity flourished.

In 2008, after a long, successful battle against his democratic rivals, in particular Hillary Clinton and the Clinton machine, Obama next faced off against his Republican challenger, Senator John McCain. After watching some of the televised debates and seeing Obama share the stage with John McCain and other Republican opponents, I was then confident that Mr. Obama was to become our forty-fourth president. Simply stated, Obama appeared and sounded more presidential.

Senator John McCain is a war hero. During the Vietnam War, he was nearly killed. He escaped serious injury on July 29, 1967, when his A-4 Skyhawk plane was accidentally shot by a missile from another plane while

118

decked on board the *USS Forrestall*, causing explosions and fires that killed 134 people.[1] On October 26, 1967, while on a bombing mission over Hanoi, he was shot down, seriously injured, and captured by the North Vietnamese. As a prisoner of war for nearly six years, John McCain was tortured several times by the enemy and repeatedly refused early repatriation. He was released from his imprisonment in 1973 and retired from the military in 1981. His war wounds left him with permanent physical limitations. McCain earned the Silver Star, Bronze Star, Purple Heart, and Distinguished Flying Cross.[2]

John McCain is also an experienced, educated politician, having served in a political office since 1982. In 1986, McCain won election to the US Senate. Both in the House and the Senate, McCain earned a reputation as a conservative politician who nonetheless was not afraid to risk challenging the ruling party. As a result he was often described as a "political maverick." [3]

However, sharing the stage with his opponent, the much younger (age forty-seven), taller, and influential speaker Senator Barak Obama made the shorter, older (age seventy-two) Senator John McCain appear frail and less electable to the office of the presidency. Obama appealed more to younger voters and to women of all ages. Because of his race alone, he represented a changing America. This aspect drew many minority groups to him. Obama had a listening audience of nearly 90 percent of voting blacks, as well as the support of many Hispanics, Latinos, and other minorities. With so many Americans tired of the same old politics and its tricky maneuvers, it was clear that Obama's time had arrived.

Obama's campaign theme was "hope and change." His message of hope was evidently necessary due to a failing economy, wars, a search for Osama bin Laden, and a lack of leadership in government. His message of change took on a grand scale, alluding to crossing racial barriers, changing political parties, reestablishing international policies, ending a war, and revamping or transforming America. This "change" was treading new waters and taking

119

our country in a different direction. This change was being proposed by and directed under the leadership of a young, handsome, intelligent, fluent black man.

In a last-ditch effort to save his presidential race for the White House, John McCain selected then-unknown Alaska Governor Sarah Palin as his running mate. Selecting a woman helped gain women voters and more conservative support. Many conservatives were not clearly behind McCain due to his reputation as a "maverick', one who was willing to take a position at odds with his party leadership, and his shared mixed values. So Sarah Palins' addition appeared to be a smart move by McCain's organization. Barack Obama had, on the other hand, selected the oft-misspoken, white, older Joe Biden over the popular, more astute Senator Hillary Clinton. This choice had offended many of his women supporters, especially white women. In fact, I remember one comedian joking about how Obama had really screwed up in picking Joe Biden as his running mate. He joked that "white women would never vote for another old white man. Once they had one old white dude, they don't want another one."

As it turned out, the one who had really screwed up was John McCain. Sarah Palin had boosted his numbers in the polls, due mainly to her winning over some women who had previously supported Barack Obama. In addition, she instantly grabbed the audience of mainstream conservatives with the support of the UMAs, Rush Limbaugh, Sean Hannity, Glenn Beck, and Mark Levin. Sarah Palin also drew a large crowed wherever and whenever she appeared on the campaign trail. But when she had interviews with the mainstream media and participated in debates, her lack of knowledge, political education, social and economic understanding exposed her in a humongous and very humorous way.

Commentators, comedians, and Democrats had a field day criticizing and making jokes and wisecracks about the comments made by Mrs. Palin and the expressions she used. In particular, the popular comedy television show *Saturday Night Live* had actress, writer, and comedian Tina Fey portrayed Sarah Palin in various skits that were

120

hysterically funny and classical. Then there was the ridiculous interview that Sarah Palin had with famed reporter Katie Couric, where Mrs. Palin describes watching Russia fly their planes over Alaska as if she were viewing it from her own backyard. Also notable is how, when asked by Katie Couric what specific newspapers or magazines she reads to keep up with world events, Mrs. Palin could not name one. In essence, Mrs. Palin was not seen by the majority of the American public as worthy of the office of vice president of the United States. As a result, John McCain and his vice presidential selection, Sarah Palin, lost miserably in a landslide defeat to Barack Obama. Therefore, the messages of "change" and "the transformation of America" had won.

On November 4, 2008, President-elect Barack Obama, with his wife Michelle by his side, made history. On center stage in Chicago's Grant Park, Obama told an estimated crowd of more than 240,000 supporters, "It has been a long time coming. Because of what we did on this day, in this election, in this defining moment, change has come to America!"

That night, I watched and recorded this event on my television. I remember thinking how much I really wish my father had been alive to have seen this momentous event. He would have never believed that such a thing could have taken place in this country. Having been raised in southern Alabama, his childhood was filled with racist hatred and discrimination. His father—my grandfather, a man whom I never knew—was tied to a railroad track and killed by a running locomotive because he was accused of having a relationship with a white woman. My dad observed discrimination firsthand from his youth up to and far into his adult life. Yet he taught us not to hate but to think, to reason, to react cautiously, and to treat others the way we wanted to be treated.

As I observed Obama's victory speech, like so many other minorities, particularly those of African-American decent, I felt a deep sense of pride and accomplishment. His audience that night was experiencing great emotion, tears of joy, and a renewed hope that had not been felt since before

121

the loss of Dr. Martin Luther King and President John F. Kennedy. The defeated John McCain was even so moved as to say, "This is a historic election, and I recognize the special significance it has for African-Americans, and for the special pride that must be theirs tonight."[4] Obama's victory was an inspirational one for a people who had suffered feeling lesser for so very long. Celebrities like Oprah Winfrey and Muhammad Ali, civil rights leaders like Reverend Jesse Jackson and Reverend Al Sharpton, and many actors, artists, entertainers, and sports stars who were in the audience that night were also moved with emotion. Now change had arrived: the forty-fourth president of the United States of America had overcome a major barrier and entered the highest office in the land. In the words of Obama, "It [had] been a long time coming."

As I mentioned in the introduction, people in general do not respond to change very well. Some have unreal expectations when change is promised. Others may look upon change pessimistically or negatively. Others welcome it, and some just watch it take place. Then there are those who say, "What the heck just happened?"

At noon on January 30, 2009, Mr. Obama was sworn into office and became President Obama. The new president acknowledged the significance of his position in a nation where race has long been a highly charged subject. Obama remarked, "A man whose father less than sixty years ago might not have been served at a local restaurant can now stand before you to take a sacred oath." Speaking about change in America, he declared, "What the cynics fail to understand is that the ground has shifted beneath them, that the stale political arguments that have consumed us for so long no longer apply." This statement later proved to be false. Perhaps President Obama himself did not fully recognize the significance of the new change that had taken place, but many of his political enemies and others certainly did. They knew exactly what the heck had just happened.

The enemies and critics of the new president knew what happened because they had observed it so many times before—not in the form of as momentous an event as a

122

black man being elected to the highest political office in the land, but as smaller changes in society over time. They had observed "change" when Ms. Parks refused to give up her seat to a white passenger on the bus, when Sidney Poitier became a leading actor in movies, when Jack Johnson became the first African-American heavyweight boxing champion, when Jackie Robinson became the first African-American to play modern Major League Baseball, and when Dr. Martin Luther King participated in victorious marches for nonviolence and equality. These and so many other great events represented African-American triumphs that changed the public's views and opinions and eventually changed our society. But the greater the change, the stronger the opposition; the bigger the cause, the harder the fight. The challenges Obama's presidency to society would prove to be no different.

The opposition to Obama—not just Republicans and conservatives, but all those who viewed the changing America as a threat to their way of life—immediately cultivated a great hatred toward the new administration. The UMAs painted Obama as anti-Christian, socialist, fascist, and communist, painting him as a man devoted to the destruction of the country and much, much more. By the end of his second year in office, President Obama had fully recognized the obvious, as is apparent from what he related to an audience in Wisconsin: "They talk about me like a dog. That's not in my prepared remarks, it's just -- but it's true."[5]

Newsone.com published an interesting article by D. L. Chandler entitled "Continued GOP Disrespect of Obama is Unacceptable." The article stated the following: "During President Barack Obama's historic rise from state Senator to the highest office in the land, he has endured relentless disrespect from his various critics on both sides of the aisle. However, nothing from the pundits and other talking heads have come close to crossing the line on the level of elected officials who represent both the GOP and the burgeoning Tea Party."[6] Former President Jimmy Carter put it this way:

I think an overwhelming portion of the intensely demonstrated animosity toward President Barack Obama is

The Ugly Mouths of America!

based on the fact that he is a black man, that he's African-American...I live in the South, and I've seen the South come a long way, and I've seen the rest of the country that shared the South's attitude toward minority groups at that time, particularly African-Americans...And that racism inclination still exists. And I think it's bubbled up to the surface because of the belief among many white people, not just in the South but around the country, that African-Americans are not qualified to lead this great country. It's an abominable circumstance, and it grieves me and concerns me very deeply.[7]

If we were to examine some of the comments made by our elected officials, we would clearly observe why former president Jimmy Carter would make such a profound statement.

Republican Colorado Congressman Doug Lamborn said, "Even if some people say, 'Well the Republicans should have done this or they should have done that,' they will hold the president responsible. Now, I don't even want to have to be associated with him. It's like touching a tar baby and you get it, you're stuck, and you're a part of the problem now and you can't get away. I don't want that to happen to us, but if it does or not, he'll still get, properly so, the blame because his policies for four years will have failed the American people."[8]

Senator Majority Leader Harry Reid privately stated that he believed Barack Obama was well suited for a presidential run because he was a "light-skinned" African-American "with no Negro dialect, unless he wanted to have one."[9]

Then there is the infamous shouting of "you lie" by Congressman Joe Wilson at the president during his address to a joint session of Congress. If this not racially oriented, it is at least definitely gross disrespect for the man and the office.

But there are far more challenges being faced by Obama than just hate speech and racism. Many question if

124

he is a socialist, a communist, or a Marxist dictator. Many ask whether he loves this country and has purposeful changes in mind for its betterment of all.

I have read Obama's book, *The Audacity of Hope* (2006), and I must admit he is a far better writer than I am. Writing about his life and experiences as a professor of law, Obama discusses our Constitution, politics, values, and opportunities, as well as race. He shares his inner thoughts, dreams, and family values. If this book were really read by all, the meaningless cry that he is a communist would clearly be dispensed with. However, he does have a unique outlook on the political system that has governed our nation for the last fifty years. He apparently believes in the government being more involved in assisting the needs of the people—not as a dictatorship, like in the case of a government ruled by a communist or Marxist, although some have called him these things, but as a government for the people and by the people. The problem is that the "people" who make up this country have changed. Now we have become enormously diversified.

Who are the people? Our nation has undergone a tremendous metaphoric change. Many did not recognize the extent of the rapid change until it climaxed with the election of a black man into the highest office in the land. When they observed a black family moving into the White House, even bringing along the family's black dog, and then remodeling and replacing antiquated pictures and inviting black athletes and rap and soul artists as guests, many had to come to grips with the fact that our great nation has changed and is forever changing.

President Obama addressed this change in his January 20, 2009, inauguration speech:

...We are a nation of Christians and Muslims, Jews and Hindus, and nonbelievers. We are shaped by every language and culture, drawn from every end of this Earth.

And because we have tasted the bitter swill of civil war and segregation and emerged from that dark chapter stronger and more united, we cannot help but believe that the old hatreds shall someday pass; that the lines of tribe shall soon dissolve; that as the world grows smaller, our common humanity shall reveal itself; and that America must play its role in ushering in a new era of peace.

To the Muslim world, we seek a new way forward, based on mutual interest and mutual respect. To those leaders around the globe who seek to sow conflict or blame their society's ills on the West, know that your people will judge you on what you can build, not what you destroy.[10]

In his first statement above, President Obama is acknowledging a fundamental change that has already taken place. Our nation's Founding Fathers, such as George Washington, John Adams, Benjamin Franklin, Alexander Hamilton, Abraham Lincoln, and Thomas Jefferson, were all white men with so-called Christian beliefs. They used Bible-based principles to assist in their writing and establishing the laws that govern us today. This is not to say that these men were true Christians or followers of Christ, but these men did recognize that "the people" of their time were a God-fearing people who regarded the Bible as a supreme authority and God's word. The second president of the United States, John Adams, summed it up by saying, "Our Constitution was made only for a moral and religious people. It is wholly inadequate to the government of any other."[11] Therefore, America was established with the overwhelming support of Christendom, and it was governed by a white majority.

Today, the dominance of the Christian religion in America has diminished. When watching television, listening to music, or surfing the Internet, one can easily observe that the vast majority of people have different mental dispositions than those of "a moral and religious people." In general, people are no longer God-fearing. To ensure your understanding of how I am using the term *God-fearing*, I would like to clarify that I am referring to a reverence and deep-rooted respect for God as the Grand Creator and instructor. (Psalms 111:10). For the most part, religious thoughts, prayers, and reverence for God have taken a back seat to individualism, accomplishment, and entitlement. A

126

belief in God is held to be personal and private, at times improper to even mention in public. The people have become, just as the president stated, "a nation of Christians and Muslims, Jews and Hindus, and nonbelievers."

Among those of us who are believers, the diversity of what we believe and practice is infinite. With so many people representing different nationalities, backgrounds, cultures, and societies, America has become a melting pot of religious practicers and atheists. No longer is America "one nation under God"; we have become one nation under the god of diversity. This god demands new rules, new laws, and a transformation of government. Whether we like it or not, President Obama represents the government of a diversified nation.

Along with becoming president at a time when so many different nationalities, cultures, ethnic backgrounds, and beliefs are prevalent, Obama adopted many of the difficult and life-threatening challenges our country is presently facing. I remember telling my wife prior to his election that I didn't know why anyone would want to occupy the office of the presidency at this time in our nation's history.

In 2011, among the many problems facing the incumbent president and America are the war on terrorism, the war in Afghanistan, the struggling global and domestic economy, the mortgage crisis, rising gas prices, a lack of jobs, health care reform, the end of social security, the development of alternative energy, undereducated children, government spending and waste, the development of a democratic government in Iraq, navigation and negotiation of China's influence, the defiance of North Korea, the reemergence of Russia, and the threat of nuclear development in Iran. There are these things and so much more for the people of a diversified nation to express their opinions on. This is also where the UMAs have an advantage.

I find it very interesting that it is easy to complain or criticize others without offering any realistic solution to a

127

problem. One can easily say what a person or group should not do and fail to offer up what should be done. The big three UMAs, Rush Limbaugh, Sean Hannity and Glenn Beck, have often expressed no interest in running for political office, yet they preach politics and spread negative propaganda daily. These UMAs who appear to hate the president and his administration go on the attack, telling viewers what is wrong—often with falsehoods and inaccuracies—and not saying what is right or good. As a result, they and other Ugly Mouths have become a resource for politicians and organizations opposed to the Obama administration, helping them reach millions of people and receive their support. This resource rakes in millions of dollars for the UMAs and millions of votes for its political accomplices.

Mr. Limbaugh was not alone in hoping Obama's presidency would fail. Right at the outset, Sean Hannity announced his campaign "Stop the Obama Express." Under Sean Hannity's picture on news talk radio website www.KRMG.com, you will find the caption "Sean Hannity | Your home for the 'Stop Obama Express.'"[12] This campaign earned Sean Hannity the title of *Media Matters'* 2008 Misinformer of the Year. This is *Media Matters'* explanation for why it gave this title to Hannity:

As Media Matters for America has demonstrated time and again, Fox News' Sean Hannity has been a prolific and influential purveyor of conservative misinformation. But never has he so enthusiastically applied his talents for spreading misinformation as he did to the 2008 presidential race, focusing his energies primarily on President-elect Barack Obama. Day after day, Hannity devoted his two Fox News shows and his three-hour ABC Radio Networks program to "demonizing" the Democratic presidential candidates, starkly explaining in August: "That's my job...I led the 'Stop Hillary Express.' By the way, now it's the 'Stop Obama Express.'" Hannity's "Stop Obama Express" promoted and embellished a vast array of misleading attacks and false claims about Obama. Along the way, he uncritically adopted and promoted countless Republican talking points and played host to numerous credibility-challenged smear

128

artists who painted Obama as a dangerous radical. When he was not going after Obama, Hannity attacked members of Obama's family, as well as Sen. Hillary Clinton and other progressives, and denied all the while that he had unfairly attacked anyone.[13]

Hannity is devoted to the failure of President Obama and the Democrats so much so that he admits that it is his job. I wonder, if Obama wins a second term does that mean that we can expect the firing of Sean Hannity?

On November 19, 2009, Glenn Beck warned Teabaggers that they must stop Obama or "face the end of America as [they] know it." Here is the transcript, as published by Daily Kos TV:

What's in this legislation? The end of America as you know it, I believe.

We are taking about massive, sweeping change. American's showed up by the hundreds of thousands at various tea parties to demand the opposite of this: stop spending money. But look at these bills. Look at this. This is a fundamental transformation of America. Massive changes to the way you live your life. The Senate plans to pass this mess before Christmas.

I don't want to believe the things I believe about what's happening in Washington, but we have a president who has surrounded himself not with free-market system lovers. These are people that don't want to increase America's prosperity, they are spending us into oblivion for their own purposes.

Obama is trying to overwhelm the system right now with massive new government takeover programs. I mean look at these bills. This is just for health care. Stimulus. This is insanity.

Obama is insisting on this all at once. His entire transformation America package all with twelve months of his administration. We are talking here America about the end of our way of life. This is not some wild conspiracy tale.

They already control our banks. They control the auto industry. Control the temperature inside of your home. Control of one-sixth of the economy. Taking over the Internet in the name of neutrality. They are moving at the speed of light and we've got to get up off of our couches and get into their offices.

If we don't stop this insanity now, they will fundamentally transform America. It must end. You must make a choice. This, or this.[14]

There is no doubt that this type of propaganda verbiage implants fear and resentment into the audience of his listeners. Beck says "this is not a wild conspiracy", but rather a take-over. His audience is made to feel that what they presently have will be taken away from them, and as a result, they must choose on the basis of patriotism.

Many members of the Republican Party, as well as some Democrats, felt the same way, believing the Obama administration must not succeed. Former Secretary of the State, General Colin Powel when interviewing with Sean Hannity, relates that after Obama was inaugurated a number of Republicans, who are his friends said, "We are going to destroy him. We are going to destroy him".[15] Making use of paid lobbyists and third-party UMAs, politicians have led a gigantic campaign to spread negative propaganda and turn the American voters against the president. This campaign has been in full force for nearly four years, and it is the source of the so-called grassroots Tea Party movement. This movement is funded and backed by the billionaire Koch brothers, who represent a major player in corporate America, along with the Heritage Group, Americans for Prosperity, and huge banking and other organizations. This conglomerate has continuously painted a very negative picture of the president and his administration in an effort to prevent America from changing. It has also resulted in gross disrespect shown toward the president and his administration, as well as mistrust of our very government.

130

Sadly, all this has come at a critical time in our nation's history.

The fundamental transformation of America is real. We must recognize that the America of the past is gone forever. New laws are evolving to fulfill the needs and wants of our new society and a forever-changing people. Here are some astounding statistics regarding America's future society:

Ethnic and racial minorities will comprise a majority of the nation's population in a little more than a generation, according to new Census Bureau projections, a transformation that is occurring faster than anticipated just a few years ago...The census calculates that by 2042, Americans who identify themselves as Hispanic, black, Asian, American Indian, Native Hawaiian and Pacific Islander will together outnumber non-Hispanic whites.[16]

So-called minorities, the Census Bureau projects, will constitute a majority of the nation's children under 18 by 2023 and of working-age Americans by 2039.[17]

For the first time, both the number and the proportion of non-Hispanic whites, who now account for 66 percent of the population, will decline, starting around 2030. By 2050, their share will dip to 46 percent."[18]

"Unauthorized immigrants living in the United States are more geographically dispersed than in the past and are more likely than either U.S. born residents or legal immigrants to live in a household with a spouse and children. In addition, a growing share of the children of unauthorized immigrant parents (73%), were born in this country and are U.S. citizens.[19]

Based on March 2008 data collected by the Census Bureau, the Center estimates that unauthorized immigrants are 4% of the nation's population and 5.4% of its workforce. Their children, both those who are unauthorized immigrants themselves and those who are U.S. citizens, make up 6.8%

of the students enrolled in the nation's elementary and secondary schools.[20]

About three-quarters (76%) of the nation's unauthorized immigrant population are Hispanics. The majority of undocumented immigrants (59%) are from Mexico, numbering 7 million. Significant regional sources of unauthorized immigrants include Asia (11%), Central America (11%), South America (7%), the Caribbean (4%) and the Middle East (less than 2%)".[21]

New minorities—Hispanics, Asians, and other groups apart from whites, blacks, and American Indians—account for all of the growth among the nation's child population. From 2000 to 2010, the population of white children nationwide declined by 4.3 million, while the population of Hispanic and Asian children grew by 5.5 million.[22]

In almost half of states and nearly one-third of large metro areas, child populations declined in the 2000s. White child populations dropped in 46 states and 86 of the 100 largest metro areas, but gains of new minority children forestalled more widespread overall declines in youth.[23]

It is the reality of these and other statistics that demand a transformation of Americans' ideologies. William Frey, a demographer at Brookings University, expressed it this way: "This is just an extraordinary explosion of diversity all across the United States."[24]

Globally, in order to remain a competitive and dominating force, international dealings with our allies must shift and peace talks with our enemies must progress. This necessitates a more cautious approach rather than quick decisions to engage in military action. The Obama administration seems to have taken this approach. Careful, consultative dialogue takes time, and it also gives the UMAs the opportunity to attack diplomatic policies and procedures. They often have a lot to say despite failing to grasp the full scope of all that is involved in making a decision for the betterment of the country and global peace.

Obama appears to have been very successful at making foreign policy. This is not to say that I agree or disagree with his foreign policies; it is just to state the obvious. Fareed Zakaria, host of CNN's international affairs program, spent several weeks preparing an essay on President Obama for *Time* magazine. In the article, Mr. Zakaria writes, "The question isn't whether Barack Obama has been a good foreign policy President. It's whether he can be a great one."[25] After stating how Obama has surrounded himself with heavyweights, including his 2008 rivals Hilary Clinton and Joe Biden, Mr. Zakaria continues,

Obama can take credit for having achieved much along these lines. But to leave a more lasting legacy than one of focus, effectiveness and good public diplomacy, he will need to build on his successes and conceive and implement a set of policies that promote a vision of a better world—more stable, more open and more free. Good foreign policy Presidents (like Dwight Eisenhower and George H.W. Bush) managed a complex set of challenges expertly, making few costly errors. Bad ones (like George W. Bush and Lyndon Johnson) made mistakes that cost America in lives, treasure and prestige. But great foreign policy Presidents (like Harry Truman) created enduring structures and relationships that produced lasting peace and prosperity. Obama has been a good foreign policy President; he has the opportunity to become a great one.[26]

In addition, President Obama has relentlessly and aggressively pursued the war on terrorism. As Fareed Zakaria reports,

[President Obama] embraced counterterrorism with ferocity, dramatically expanding the campaign of special operations and drone attacks that have since killed most of al-Qaeda's senior leaders—almost all of whom lived in Pakistan. The crowning success of this strategy was the raid on Osama bin Laden's compound in Pakistan and his assassination. (Of course, as with all successful counterterrorism, the strategy seems foolproof in retrospect. Had these various missions failed, had many American soldiers died, those tactics would have been called dangerous and foolhardy.) In the central

133

battle in the war on terrorism, Obama adopted many of the Bush Administration's aggressive tactics, used them more aggressively and achieved greater success.[27]

The UMAs never seem to talk about these pivotal victories and successes.

Shortly before midnight on May 1, 2011, President Barack Obama announced on nationwide television the death of Osama bin Laden, the long-hunted leader of al-Qaeda and mastermind behind the terrorist acts of September 11, 2001. These attacks were the worst ever on American soil, killing over three thousand people. Thus, President Obama said that the killing of bin Laden was "the most significant achievement to date" in the war against al-Qaeda.

Obama's brief speech gave us a few details on the operations that led America's Special Forces to find and kill Osama bin Laden. Obama described how US intelligence operations received information in August 2010 about the location of Osama bin Laden. This ultimately led to the authorization of a small team of American forces to conduct an operation targeting bin Laden. After a firefight, our forces killed bin Laden and took possession of his body. The president also reported that precautionary measures had been taken to prevent civilian casualties and that there were, furthermore, no American casualties. The president emphasized that Americans "did not choose this fight" against al-Qaeda but rather that "it came to our shores." In addition, he praised US military and intelligence professionals for working together tirelessly to achieve this goal. To the families who lost loved ones in the terrorist attacks of 9/11, he said the United States "has never forgotten" their losses and that "justice has been done."

I remember listening to this major announcement and thinking it was a huge bump for President Obama's place in history and perhaps also for his run for a second presidential term. It had been nearly ten years since President George W. Bush had announced he was going to find and capture or kill the al-Qaeda leader in our war

134

against terrorism. On September 17, 2001, Bush had said, in answer to a question poised to him regarding bin Laden's capture or death, "I want justice. There is an old poster out west as I recall, that said wanted dead or alive."[28] During an unannounced visit to Afghanistan nearly five years later, on May 2, 2006, Bush again vowed to capture Osama bin Laden and Taliban ruler Mullah Mohammed Omar: "It's not a matter of if they're captured or brought to justice, it's when they're brought to justice."[29] Bush was right on par with regard to bringing bin Laden to justice, except that it wasn't accomplished during his eight years in office.

As I watched President Obama's announcement from the White House, I couldn't help but wonder how the UMAs would spin this one. How could you turn the positive news of the death of the best-known terrorist in the world—a man who has been hunted for nearly a decade—into a criticism of the president? Unsurprisingly, however, they quickly found a way to spin it.

The UMAs wanted to give the credit to the previous administration, particularly former president George W. Bush, who had searched for bin Laden for nearly seven years. They criticized Obama for giving too much credit to his administration and US intelligence and not enough to the US Special Forces who had accomplished the work with their own sweat and blood. Rush Limbaugh was so picky that he was apparently counting President Obama's words: "For the record ladies and gentlemen, in his brief announcement last night, President Obama used the word 'I' ten times, the word 'me' three times, the word 'mine' five times, and the word 'my' three times."[30]

How much more ridiculous could Mr. Limbaugh become? So it is with any man-made organization that credit is given to the one in charge, the commander-in-chief. Does Mr. Limbaugh think only Thomas Edison worked on the lightbulb or only Henry Ford designed the automobile? Maybe he thinks Thomas Jefferson was the only one who worked on the Declaration of Independence or that George Washington was victorious in the American Revolution all by himself. No, these things are not true, but these men were

135

the leaders of their time, and history credits them with those great accomplishments and victories.

When Rush was talking about Obama's historic feat on the air, for the next few days he would often misspeak, saying "the death of Obama" instead of "the death of Osama." Each time he did this, of course, he would correct himself and claim he hadn't done it on purpose. Whether it was deliberate or not, he was deviously communicating a different thought: in a sublime yet subtle way, he was announcing the death of the president of the United States.

Because Rush is a seasoned radio personality who has been on the air for over twenty years, I'm convinced this couldn't have been a continuous mistake. This is a clear example of the Rush Limbaugh way of promoting confrontational entertainment. There was a simple fix that could have corrected this problem: Rush simply needed to say "President Obama" in full whenever referring to the president.

Sean Hannity gave the news of the death of bin Laden a slightly different spin. He gave the president "lots of credit" and said it was a "gutsy" move to send American forces in to accomplish this feat. But then the spin came when Hannity said, "President Obama did almost the opposite of what candidate Obama said he would do."[31] This wasn't true. During a national television debate against Senator John McCain in 2008, Senator Obama boldly said, "We will kill Bin Laden. We will crush al-Qaeda."[32]

There were many other ways the UMAs sought to twist the positive news of bin Laden's death. Some said that without the use of tactics like waterboarding and other methods of torture to gather information, the Obama administration would not have obtained the intelligence telling it where bin Laden was hiding. Others said it was Bush's methods that had really been used to find him and that the former president should be given the credit. But the bottom line is, like it or not, President Obama will get the credit—he will go down in history as the one who ordered the killing of the terrorist Osama bin Laden.

136

Viewing it from a different perspective, what if the mission had been a failure? Let's say the chopper crashed, the Special Forces personnel were captured or killed, and Osama bin Laden escaped completely unharmed. Do you think for one moment they would have blamed George Bush's tactics or the US forces for the failed mission? The blame would have gone straight to President Obama, his administration, and its intelligence-reporting personnel. Just as the old saying goes, if the shoe fits, wear it. Good or bad, the leader gets the credit or the blame.

In the days after the death of bin Laden, some of the UMAs started saying "we need to see the body" and "show us the photos of his corpse." Sean Hannity was clearly frustrated with the Obama administration for its reluctance to publish bin Laden's death pictures.

History has shown with nearly every major success a man or woman has is preceded or accompanied by some failures. This is true of President Obama and his administration. For example, we have the failed government-funded energy companies, such as Solyndra, Beacon Power, and EnerDel, which combined received hundreds of millions of dollars in an effort to expand the program outlined by Obama's Recovery Act. For these government-funded failures, Obama and his Energy Department should have and did receive the reproof of an angry people. It was an irresponsible handling of taxpayers' moneys. Rightfully so, the UMAs were relentless in exposing these errors in government funding. However, the UMAs failed to speak about other efforts made by Obama that were successful, such the bailout of some banks and the funding of GMAC and Chrysler. Credit should be given where credit is due.

Time magazine writer, Michael Grunwald, published a very interesting article entitled, "How the Stimulus Is Changing America". In his article Grunwald relates how the American Recovery and Reinvestment Act of 2009 was more than just a jobs bill. Although Republicans mock it as, "a Big Government boondoggle" the stimulus has cut taxes for 95% of working Americans, bailed out every state, hustled record amounts of unemployment benefits and other

137

aid to struggling families and funded more than 100,000 projects to upgrade roads, subways, schools, airports, military bases and much more. [33] On a negative note, this bill was passed with a $787 billion dollar price tag!

Michael Grunwald states many benefits to the stimulus that is not often mentioned by the UMAs. But the stimulus indicates major changes to help America continue to compete on a global scale and move forward in technology for the twenty first century. He continues:

The stimulus is also stocked with non-energy game changers, like a tenfold increase in funding to expand access to broadband and an effort to sequence more than 2,300 complete human genomes — when only 34 were sequenced with all previous aid. There's $8 billion for a high-speed passenger rail network, the boldest federal transportation initiative since the interstate highways. There's $4.35 billion in Race to the Top grants to promote accountability in public schools, perhaps the most significant federal education initiative ever — it's already prompted 35 states and the District of Columbia to adopt reforms to qualify for the cash. There's $20 billion to move health records into the digital age, which should reduce redundant tests, dangerous drug interactions and errors caused by doctors with chicken-scratch handwriting.[34]

As I finish writing this, the 2012 presidential campaign is starting to heat up. I believe the main opponent of Obama will be Senator Mitt Romney. Can Romney actually beat Obama and become the forty-fifth president of the United States? I don't know. I do think Obama is beatable, but it will not be an easy task. It is not Mitt Romney that might beat President Obama—it's the poor economy.

Along with a high unemployment rate of over 8 percent, there is another major obstacle that could cause President Obama to lose his bid for a second term: the upward climb of the price of gas.

We were very glad to hear that Osama bin Laden, a major leader of al-Qaeda, had been killed. It was good news

138

to report that all the soldiers have come home from Iraq (although some of them have being exported to Afghanistan). Also, Economists have reported that we are making some economic progress and slowly recovering from a great recession. But what affects voters the most and what they tend to remember the most at the time of an election is the condition of their financials and their ability to earn.

A May 2011 *USA Today/Gallup* poll reported that 54 percent of Americans believe that high gas prices are here to stay. In addition, the poll showed that nearly seven in ten Americans say the high cost of gasoline is causing financial hardship for their families.[35]

The price we are paying at the pump, which, according to the May 2011 article, has risen 38% over last year averages to an average of $3.96 per regular gallon. In seven states, gas prices have passed July 2008's record of $4.11 a gallon.[36] Americans shake their heads in disgust when filling up their gas tanks in order to take care of their family obligations and, for those of us who have jobs, to continue to drive to and from work. But when it costs upwards of or seventy dollars or more to fill up a car and especially if your family has more than one vehicle, it can quickly take its toll on the family's finances.

With gas prices at four-plus dollars per gallon, consumers tend to drive less, shop less, and decrease their outdoor entertainment and recreational activities. As a result, retailers, restaurants, and the recreational, entertainment, and transportation industries are forced to try to offset their losses. This is accomplished by increasing prices or decreasing workers. As the gas prices go up, then, the economy goes down. The bottom line is that unless gas prices go down, the president is in mortal peril.

The American people realize there may not be a quick solution to this problem and that gas prices started rising during the eight years of the George W. Bush presidency. But to say that "there's not much we can do next week or two weeks from now" and to advise people to "trade in an 8-mile-per gallon"[37] beater for a fuel-efficient car is not

139

good enough to win back American voters. If you could afford to buy a new car for a modest $30,000, then you would likely be able to pay four dollars at the pump. It's a simple mathematical calculation. You either have $30,000 extra cash in the bank or somewhere else, or you are making car payments of at least $325 or more per month. That averages to more than eighty dollars per week. Therefore, just say good-bye to the savings from less gas consumption.

Reality simply suggests that if President Obama, his administration, his Energy Department, or anyone else for that matter can drive gas prices down, the number of votes for Obama at the polls will go up.

I want to conclude this chapter with a vision Obama expressed in Osawatomie, Kansas, on December 6, 2011. It is my humble opinion that this vision clearly speaks about the man that many of us feel we do not know. Perhaps this speech should be given more often or given more public exposure. But this is the vision of Obama's America:

Good afternoon. I want to start by thanking a few of the folks who've joined us today. We've got the mayor of Osawatomie, Phil Dudley; your superintendent, Gary French; the principal of Osawatomie High, Doug Chisam. And I've brought your former governor, who's now doing an outstanding job as our Secretary of Health and Human Services, Kathleen Sebelius.

It is great to be back in the state of Kansas. As many of you know, I've got roots here. I'm sure you're all familiar with the Obamas of Osawatomie. Actually, I like to say that I got my name from my father, but I got my accent – and my values – from my mother. She was born in Wichita. Her mother grew up in Augusta. And her father was from El Dorado. So my Kansas roots run deep.

My grandparents served during World War II -- he as a soldier in Patton's Army, she as a worker on a bomber assembly line. Together, they shared the optimism of a nation that triumphed over a Depression and fascism. They

140

believed in an America where hard work paid off, responsibility was rewarded, and anyone could make it if they tried -- no matter who you were, where you came from, or how you started out.

These values gave rise to the largest middle class and the strongest economy the world has ever known. It was here, in America, that the most productive workers and innovative companies turned out the best products on Earth, and every American shared in that pride and success -- from those in executive suites to middle management to those on the factory floor. If you gave it your all, you'd take enough home to raise your family, send your kids to school, have your health care covered, and put a little away for retirement.

Today, we are still home to the world's most productive workers and innovative companies. But for most Americans, the basic bargain that made this country great has eroded. Long before the recession hit, hard work stopped paying off for too many people. Fewer and fewer of the folks who contributed to the success of our economy actually benefitted from that success. Those at the very top grew wealthier from their incomes and investments than ever before. But everyone else struggled with costs that were growing and paychecks that weren't – and too many families found themselves racking up more and more debt just to keep up.

For many years, credit cards and home equity loans papered over the harsh realities of this new economy. But in 2008, the house of cards collapsed. We all know the story by now: Mortgages sold to people who couldn't afford them, or sometimes even understand them. Banks and investors allowed to keep packaging the risk and selling it off. Huge bets – and huge bonuses – made with other people's money on the line. Regulators who were supposed to warn us about the dangers of all this, but looked the other way or didn't have the authority to look at all.

It was wrong. It combined the breathtaking greed of a few with irresponsibility across the system. And it plunged our economy and the world into a crisis from which we are still

141

fighting to recover. It claimed the jobs, homes, and the basic security of millions – innocent, hard-working Americans who had met their responsibilities, but were still left holding the bag.

Ever since, there has been a raging debate over the best way to restore growth and prosperity; balance and fairness. Throughout the country, it has sparked protests and political movements – from the Tea Party to the people who have been occupying the streets of New York and other cities. It's left Washington in a near-constant state of gridlock. And it's been the topic of heated and sometimes colorful discussion among the men and women who are running for president.

But this isn't just another political debate. This is the defining issue of our time. This is a make or break moment for the middle class, and all those who are fighting to get into the middle class. At stake is whether this will be a country where working people can earn enough to raise a family, build a modest savings, own a home, and secure their retirement.

Now, in the midst of this debate, there are some who seem to be suffering from a kind of collective amnesia. After all that's happened, after the worst economic crisis since the Great Depression, they want to return to the same practices that got us into this mess. In fact, they want to go back to the same policies that have stacked the deck against middle-class Americans for too many years. Their philosophy is simple: we are better off when everyone is left to fend for themselves and play by their own rules.

Well, I'm here to say they are wrong. I'm here to reaffirm my deep conviction that we are greater together than we are on our own. I believe that this country succeeds when everyone gets a fair shot, when everyone does their fair share, and when everyone plays by the same rules. Those aren't Democratic or Republican values; 1% values or 99% values. They're American values, and we have to reclaim them.

You see, this isn't the first time America has faced this choice. At the turn of the last century, when a nation of farmers was transitioning to become the world's industrial

142

giant, we had to decide: would we settle for a country where most of the new railroads and factories were controlled by a few giant monopolies that kept prices high and wages low? Would we allow our citizens and even our children to work ungodly hours in conditions that were unsafe and unsanitary? Would we restrict education to the privileged few? Because some people thought massive inequality and exploitation was just the price of progress.

Theodore Roosevelt disagreed. He was the Republican son of a wealthy family. He praised what the titans of industry had done to create jobs and grow the economy. He believed then what we know is true today: that the free market is the greatest force for economic progress in human history. It's led to a prosperity and standard of living unmatched by the rest of the world.

But Roosevelt also knew that the free market has never been a free license to take whatever you want from whoever you can. It only works when there are rules of the road to ensure that competition is fair, open, and honest. And so he busted up monopolies, forcing those companies to compete for customers with better services and better prices. And today, they still must. He fought to make sure businesses couldn't profit by exploiting children, or selling food or medicine that wasn't safe. And today, they still can't.

In 1910, Teddy Roosevelt came here, to Osawatomie, and laid out his vision for what he called a New Nationalism. "Our country," he said, "...means nothing unless it means the triumph of a real democracy...of an economic system under which each man shall be guaranteed the opportunity to show the best that there is in him."

For this, Roosevelt was called a radical, a socialist, even a communist. But today, we are a richer nation and a stronger democracy because of what he fought for in his last campaign: an eight hour work day and a minimum wage for women; insurance for the unemployed, the elderly, and

143

those with disabilities; political reform and a progressive income tax.

Today, over one hundred years later, our economy has gone through another transformation. Over the last few decades, huge advances in technology have allowed businesses to do more with less, and made it easier for them to set up shop and hire workers anywhere in the world. And many of you know firsthand the painful disruptions this has caused for a lot of Americans.

Factories where people thought they would retire suddenly picked up and went overseas, where the workers were cheaper. Steel mills that needed 1,000 employees are now able to do the same work with 100, so that layoffs were too often permanent, not just a temporary part of the business cycle. These changes didn't just affect blue-collar workers. If you were a bank teller or a phone operator or a travel agent, you saw many in your profession replaced by ATMs or the internet. Today, even higher-skilled jobs like accountants and middle management can be outsourced to countries like China and India. And if you're someone whose job can be done cheaper by a computer or someone in another country, you don't have a lot of leverage with your employer when it comes to asking for better wages and benefits – especially since fewer Americans today are part of a union.

Now, just as there was in Teddy Roosevelt's time, there's been a certain crowd in Washington for the last few decades who respond to this economic challenge with the same old tune. "The market will take care of everything," they tell us. If only we cut more regulations and cut more taxes – especially for the wealthy – our economy will grow stronger. Sure, there will be winners and losers. But if the winners do really well, jobs and prosperity will eventually trickle down to everyone else. And even if prosperity doesn't trickle down, they argue, that's the price of liberty.

It's a simple theory – one that speaks to our rugged individualism and healthy skepticism of too much government. It fits well on a bumper sticker. Here's the problem: It doesn't work. It's never worked. It didn't work

144

when it was tried in the decade before the Great Depression. It's not what led to the incredible post-war boom of the 50s and 60s. And it didn't work when we tried it during the last decade.

Remember that in those years, in 2001 and 2003, Congress passed two of the most expensive tax cuts for the wealthy in history, and what did they get us? The slowest job growth in half a century. Massive deficits that have made it much harder to pay for the investments that built this country and provided the basic security that helped millions of Americans reach and stay in the middle class – things like education and infrastructure; science and technology; Medicare and Social Security.

Remember that in those years, thanks to some of the same folks who are running Congress now, we had weak regulation and little oversight, and what did that get us? Insurance companies that jacked up people's premiums with impunity, and denied care to the patients who were sick. Mortgage lenders that tricked families into buying homes they couldn't afford. A financial sector where irresponsibility and lack of basic oversight nearly destroyed our entire economy.

We simply cannot return to this brand of your-on-your-own economics if we're serious about rebuilding the middle class in this country. We know that it doesn't result in a strong economy. It results in an economy that invests too little in its people and its future. It doesn't result in a prosperity that trickles down. It results in a prosperity that's enjoyed by fewer and fewer of our citizens.

Look at the statistics. In the last few decades, the average income of the top one percent has gone up by more than 250%, to $1.2 million per year. For the top one hundredth of one percent, the average income is now $27 million per year. The typical CEO who used to earn about 30 times more than his or her workers now earns 110 times more. And yet, over the last decade, the incomes of most Americans have actually fallen by about six percent.

The Ugly Mouths of America!

This kind of inequality – a level we haven't seen since the Great Depression – hurts us all. When middle-class families can no longer afford to buy the goods and services that businesses are selling, it drags down the entire economy, from top to bottom. America was built on the idea of broad-based prosperity – that's why a CEO like Henry Ford made it his mission to pay his workers enough so that they could buy the cars they made. It's also why a recent study showed that countries with less inequality tend to have stronger and steadier economic growth over the long run.

Inequality also distorts our democracy. It gives an outsized voice to the few who can afford high-priced lobbyists and unlimited campaign contributions, and runs the risk of selling out our democracy to the highest bidder. And it leaves everyone else rightly suspicious that the system in Washington is rigged against them – that our elected representatives aren't looking out for the interests of most Americans.

More fundamentally, this kind of gaping inequality gives lie to the promise at the very heart of America: that this is the place where you can make it if you try. We tell people that in this country, even if you're born with nothing, hard work can get you into the middle class; and that your children will have the chance to do even better than you. That's why immigrants from around the world flocked to our shores.

And yet, over the last few decades, the rungs on the ladder of opportunity have grown farther and farther apart, and the middle class has shrunk. A few years after World War II, a child who was born into poverty had a slightly better than 50-50 chance of becoming middle class as an adult. By 1980, that chance fell to around 40%. And if the trend of rising inequality over the last few decades continues, it's estimated that a child born today will only have a 1 in 3 chance of making it to the middle class.

It's heartbreaking enough that there are millions of working families in this country who are now forced to take their children to food banks for a decent meal. But the idea that those children might not have a chance to climb out of that

146

situation and back into the middle class, no matter how hard they work? That's inexcusable. It's wrong. It flies in the face of everything we stand for.

Fortunately, that's not a future we have to accept. Because there's another view about how we build a strong middle class in this country – a view that's truer to our history; a vision that's been embraced by people of both parties for more than two hundred years.

It's not a view that we should somehow turn back technology or put up walls around America. It's not a view that says we should punish profit or success or pretend that government knows how to fix all society's problems. It's a view that says in America, we are greater together – when everyone engages in fair play, everyone gets a fair shot, everyone does their fair share.

So what does that mean for restoring middle-class security in today's economy?

It starts by making sure that everyone in America gets a fair shot at success. The truth is, we'll never be able to compete with other countries when it comes to who's best at letting their businesses pay the lowest wages or pollute as much as they want. That's a race to the bottom that we can't win – and shouldn't want to win. Those countries don't have a strong middle-class. They don't have our standard of living.

The race we want to win – the race we can win – is a race to the top; the race for good jobs that pay well and offer middle-class security. Businesses will create those jobs in countries with the highest-skilled, highest-educated workers; the most advanced transportation and communication; the strongest commitment to research and technology.

The world is shifting to an innovation economy. And no one does innovation better than America. No one has better colleges and universities. No one has a greater diversity of talent and ingenuity. No one's workers or entrepreneurs are more driven or daring. The things that have always been our

147

strengths match up perfectly with the demands of this moment.

But we need to meet the moment. We need to up our game. And we need to remember that we can only do that together.

It starts by making education a national mission – government and businesses; parents and citizens. In this economy, a higher education is the surest route to the middle class. The unemployment rate for Americans with a college degree or more is about half the national average. Their income is twice as high as those who don't have a high school diploma. We shouldn't be laying off good teachers right now – we should be hiring them. We shouldn't be expecting less of our schools – we should be demanding more. We shouldn't be making it harder to afford college – we should be a country where everyone has the chance to go.

In today's innovation economy, we also need a world-class commitment to science, research, and the next generation of high-tech manufacturing. Our factories and their workers shouldn't be idle. We should be giving people the chance to get new skills and training at community colleges, so they can learn to make wind turbines and semiconductors and high-powered batteries. And by the way – if we don't have an economy built on bubbles and financial speculation, our best and brightest won't all gravitate towards careers in banking and finance. Because if we want an economy that's built to last, we need more of those young people in science and engineering. This country shouldn't be known for bad debt and phony profits. We should be known for creating and selling products all over the world that are stamped with three proud words: Made in America.

Today, manufacturers and other companies are setting up shop in places with the best infrastructure to ship their products, move their workers, and communicate with the rest of the world. That's why the over one million construction workers who lost their jobs when the housing market collapsed shouldn't be sitting at home with nothing to do. They should be rebuilding our roads and bridges; laying

148

down faster railroads and broadband; modernizing our schools – all the things other countries are already doing to attract good jobs and businesses to their shores.

Yes, businesses, not government, will always be the primary generator of good jobs with incomes that lift people into the middle class and keep them there. But as a nation, we have always come together, through our government, to help create the conditions where both workers and businesses can succeed. Historically, that hasn't been a partisan idea. Franklin Roosevelt worked with Democrats and Republicans to give veterans of World War II, including my grandfather, the chance to go to college on the GI Bill. It was Republican President Dwight Eisenhower, a proud son of Kansas, who started the interstate highway system and doubled-down on science and research to stay ahead of the Soviets.

Of course, those productive investments cost money. And so we've also paid for these investments by asking everyone to do their fair share. If we had unlimited resources, no one would ever have to pay any taxes and we'd never have to cut any spending. But we don't have unlimited resources. And so we have to set priorities. If we want a strong middle class, then our tax code must reflect our values. We have to make choices.

Today that choice is very clear. To reduce our deficit, I've already signed nearly $1 trillion of spending cuts into law, and proposed trillions more – including reforms that would lower the cost of Medicare and Medicaid.

But in order to actually close the deficit and get our fiscal house in order, we have to decide what our priorities are. Most immediately, we need to extend a payroll tax cut that's set to expire at the end of this month. If we don't do that, 160 million Americans will see their taxes go up by an average of $1,000, and it would badly weaken our recovery.

But in the long term, we have to rethink our tax system more fundamentally. We have to ask ourselves: Do we want to make the investments we need in things like education, and research, and high-tech manufacturing? Or do we want to

The Ugly Mouths of America!

keep in place the tax breaks for the wealthiest Americans in our country? Because we can't afford to do both. That's not politics. That's just math.

So far, most of the Republicans in Washington have refused, under any circumstances, to ask the wealthiest Americans to go the same tax rates they were paying when Bill Clinton was president.

Now, keep in mind, when President Clinton first proposed these tax increases, folks in Congress predicted they would kill jobs and lead to another recession. Instead, our economy created nearly 23 million jobs and we eliminated the deficit. Today, the wealthiest Americans are paying the lowest taxes in over half a century. This isn't like in the early 50s, when the top tax rate was over 90%, or even the early 80s, when it was about 70%. Under President Clinton, the top rate was only about 39%. Today, thanks to loopholes and shelters, a quarter of all millionaires now pay lower tax rates than millions of middle-class households. Some billionaires have a tax rate as low as 1%. One percent.

This is the height of unfairness. It is wrong that in the United States of America, a teacher or a nurse or a construction worker who earns $50,000 should pay a higher tax rate than somebody pulling in $50 million. It is wrong for Warren Buffett's secretary to pay a higher tax rate than Warren Buffett. And he agrees with me. So do most Americans – Democrats, Independents, and Republicans. And I know that many of our wealthiest citizens would agree to contribute a little more if it meant reducing the deficit and strengthening the economy that made their success possible.

This isn't about class warfare. This is about the nation's welfare. It's about making choices that benefit not just the people who've done fantastically well over the last few decades, but that benefits the middle class, and those fighting to get to the middle class, and the economy as a whole.

Finally, a strong middle class can only exist in an economy where everyone plays by the same rules, from Wall Street to

150

Main Street. As infuriating as it was for all of us, we rescued our major banks from collapse, not only because a full blown financial meltdown would have sent us into a second Depression, but because we need a strong, healthy financial sector in this country.

But part of the deal was that we would not go back to business as usual. That's why last year we put in place new rules of the road that refocus the financial sector on this core purpose: getting capital to the entrepreneurs with the best ideas, and financing to millions of families who want to buy a home or send their kids to college. We're not all the way there yet, and the banks are fighting us every inch of the way. But already, some of these reforms are being implemented. If you're a big bank or risky financial institution, you'll have to write out a "living will" that details exactly how you'll pay the bills if you fail, so that taxpayers are never again on the hook for Wall Street's mistakes. There are also limits on the size of banks and new abilities for regulators to dismantle a firm that goes under. The new law bans banks from making risky bets with their customers' deposits, and takes away big bonuses and paydays from failed CEOs, while giving shareholders a say on executive salaries.

All that is being put in place as we speak. Now, unless you're a financial institution whose business model is built on breaking the law, cheating consumers, or making risky bets that could damage the entire economy, you have nothing to fear from these new rules. My grandmother worked as a banker for most of her life, and I know that the vast majority of bankers and financial service professionals want to do right by their customers. They want to have rules in place that don't put them at a disadvantage for doing the right thing. And yet, Republicans in Congress are already fighting as hard as they can to make sure these rules aren't enforced.

I'll give you one example. For the first time in history, the reform we passed puts in place a consumer watchdog who is charged with protecting everyday Americans from being taken advantage of by mortgage lenders, payday lenders or debt collectors. The man we nominated for the post, Richard

The Ugly Mouths of America!

Cordray, is a former Attorney General of Ohio who has the support of most Attorneys General, both Democrat and Republican, throughout the country.

But the Republicans in the Senate refuse to let him do his job. Why? Does anyone here think the problem that led to our financial crisis was too much oversight of mortgage lenders or debt collectors? Of course not. Every day we go without a consumer watchdog in place is another day when a student, or a senior citizen, or member of our Armed Forces could be tricked into a loan they can't afford – something that happens all the time. Financial institutions have plenty of lobbyists looking out for their interests. Consumers deserve to have someone whose job it is to look out for them. I intend to make sure they do, and I will veto any effort to delay, defund, or dismantle the new rules we put in place.

We shouldn't be weakening oversight and accountability. We should be strengthening them. Here's another example. Too often, we've seen Wall Street firms violating major anti-fraud laws because the penalties are too weak and there's no price for being a repeat offender. No more. I'll be calling for legislation that makes these penalties count – so that firms don't see punishment for breaking the law as just the price of doing business.

The fact is, this crisis has left a deficit of trust between Main Street and Wall Street. And major banks that were rescued by the taxpayers have an obligation to go the extra mile in helping to close that deficit. At minimum, they should be remedying past mortgage abuses that led to the financial crisis, and working to keep responsible homeowners in their home. We're going to keep pushing them to provide more time for unemployed homeowners to look for work without having to worry about immediately losing their house. The big banks should increase access to refinancing opportunities to borrowers who have yet to benefit from historically low interest rates. And they should recognize that precisely because these steps are in the interest of middle-class families and the broader economy, they will also be in the banks' own long-term financial interest.

152

Investing in things like education that give everybody a chance to succeed. A tax code that makes sure everybody pays their fair share. And laws that make sure everybody follows the rules. That's what will transform our economy. That's what will grow our middle class again. In the end, rebuilding this economy based on fair play, a fair shot, and a fair share will require all of us to see the stake we have in each other's success. And it will require all of us to take some responsibility to that success.

It will require parents to get more involved in their children's education, students to study harder, and some workers to start studying all over again. It will require greater responsibility from homeowners to not take out mortgages they can't afford, and remember that if something seems too good to be true, it probably is.

It will require those of us in public service to make government more efficient, effective, and responsive to people's needs. That's why we're cutting programs we don't need, to pay for those we do. That's why we've made hundreds of regulatory reforms that will save businesses billions of dollars. That's why we're not just throwing money at education, but challenging schools to come up with the most innovative reforms and the best results.

And it will require American business leaders to understand that their obligations don't just end with their shareholders. Andy Grove, the former CEO of Intel put it best: "There's another obligation I feel personally," he said, "given that everything I've achieved in my career and a lot of what Intel has achieved…were made possible by a climate of democracy, an economic climate and investment climate provided by…the United States."

This broader obligation can take different forms. At a time when the cost of hiring workers in China is rising rapidly, it should mean more CEOs deciding that it's time to bring jobs back to the United States – not just because it's good for business, but because it's good for the country that made their business and their personal success possible.

153

I think about the Big Three Auto companies who, during recent negotiations, agreed to create more jobs and cars in America; who decided to give bonuses, not just to their executives, but to all their employees – so that everyone was invested in the company's success.

I think about a company based in Warroad, Minnesota called Marvin Windows and Doors. During the recession, Marvin's competitors closed dozens of plants and let go hundreds of workers. But Marvin didn't lay off a single one of their four thousand or so employees. In fact, they've only laid off workers once in over a hundred years. Mr. Marvin's grandfather even kept his eight employees during the Depression.

When times get tough, the workers agree to give up some perks and pay, and so do the owners. As one owner said, "You can't grow if you're cutting your lifeblood – and that's the skills and experience your workforce delivers." For the CEO, it's about the community: "These are people we went to school with," he said. "We go to church with them. We see them in the same restaurant. Indeed, a lot of us have married local girls and boys. We could be anywhere. But we are in Warroad."

That's how America was built. That's why we're the greatest nation on Earth. That's what our greatest companies understand. Our success has never just been about survival of the fittest. It's been about building a nation where we're all better off. We pull together, we pitch in, and we do our part, believing that hard work will pay off; that responsibility will be rewarded; and that our children will inherit a nation where those values live on.

And it is that belief that rallied thousands of Americans to Osawatomie – maybe even some of your ancestors – on a rain-soaked day more than a century ago. By train, by wagon, on buggy, bicycle, and foot, they came to hear the vision of a man who loved this country, and was determined to perfect it.

154

"We are all Americans," Teddy Roosevelt told them that day. "Our common interests are as broad as the continent." In the final years of his life, Roosevelt took that same message all across this country, from tiny Osawatomie to the heart of New York City, believing that no matter where he went, or who he was talking to, all would benefit from a country in which everyone gets a fair chance.

Well into our third century as a nation, we have grown and changed in many ways since Roosevelt's time. The world is faster. The playing field is larger. The challenges are more complex.

But what hasn't changed – what can never change – are the values that got us this far. We still have a stake in each other's success. We still believe that this should be a place where you can make it if you try. And we still believe, in the words of the man who called for a New Nationalism all those years ago, "The fundamental rule in our national life – the rule which underlies all others – is that, on the whole, and in the long run, we shall go up or down together."

I believe America is on its way up. Thank you, God bless you, and may God bless the United States of America.[38]

The Ugly Mouths of America!

Chapter 8: Thoughts of Gabby

In my introduction, I informed you of the shocking and horrendous crime that took place in Tucson, Arizona, on January 8, 2011. Democratic Congresswoman Gabrielle Giffords, also known as Gabby, suffered a traumatic, life-threatening head wound when she was shot at point-blank range by a twenty-two-year-old gunman. This crazed gunman, Jared Lee Loughner, opened fire with a 9mm pistol at a shopping center where Gabby and other politicians were meeting for their semiregular community event. The gunman walked up to them while they were sitting at a table and opened fire. Gabby was the first one shot. He fired thirty-two shots in a span of fifteen seconds. Thirteen people, including Gabby, were wounded by the shooting rampage. Six were left dead, including a federal judge, John Roll, and a nine-year-old girl, Christina Green.

If you can even envision the scene, bodies were laying everywhere, and people were running for their lives, trying to find safety. On the ground, in the middle of the bodies—some wounded, some dead, and others seeking safety—Gabby, a forty-one-year-old congresswoman, was bleeding heavily from a gunshot wound to the head. As she slumped to the ground, staff members rushed to her aid. Some of those staff members were wounded, but they continued to try to help Gabby. The bullet had entered her skull right above the left eye and exited out the back of her head. It was complete chaos. As the gunman went to reload his weapon, he was taken down by a bystander and finally apprehended by the police.

Gabby was placed on a stretcher by medical professionals and airlifted to the University Medical Center in Tucson. There she was immediately operated on by a team of neurosurgeons. In order to relieve pressure on her brain, which had swelled due to the injury, the surgeons performed a decompressive craniectomy, removing a large part of Gifford's skull. According to Dr. Peter Rhee, the medical director of the hospital's trauma and critical care unit, the congresswoman was shot once in the head, with the bullet

156

going through her brain.[1] On January 9, she was announced to be alive but in critical condition.

The total damage to her brain was not made known, but the bullet had traveled through the section of the brain that controls language, vision, and the right side of the body. Gabby was put in an induced coma to help doctors monitor the traumatic brain injury and the shock to her body.

According to the *New York Post*, when Spencer Giffords, the congresswoman's father, was asked if Gabrielle had any enemies, he responded, "Yeah...the whole Tea Party." Mr. Giffords sadly expressed how "they are always getting threat[ened]."[2]

Why the threats? Like many other Democrats, Gabrielle Giffords was threatened after the passage of Obama's health care reform bill in March 2010. She also held a strong position on illegal immigration, which was a major issue in the Arizona media. She is a Democratic congresswoman, and the far right and the conservative Tea Party movement often blame politicians like her for destroying our country.

Arizona sheriff Clarence Dupnick, who coordinated the investigation of the shooting with the FBI, said Arizona has "become a Mecca for prejudice and bigotry" and that "political vitriol" may have been the reason for the shooting.[3] He urged Americans to do some serious soul-searching. He told reporters, "There's reason to believe that this individual may have a mental issue. And I think people who are unbalanced are especially susceptible to vitriol...People tend to pooh-pooh this business about all the vitriol we hear inflaming the American public by people who make a living off of doing that. That may be free speech, but it's not without consequences."[4]

There was no clear evidence indicating why this unbalanced shooter, Jared Lee Loughner, went on this death rampage; however, it appeared that Gabrielle Giffords was the main target.

157

Ex-governor of Alaska, former vice presidential candidate selection of John McCain, and major Tea Party figure Sarah Palin received a lot of criticism from the public for her infamous "crosshairs" map advertisement. This ad, featured on her website, www.Sarahpac.com, showed a map of the United States and twenty districts she was aiming to win back. Her advertisement's main slogan was "Don't get demoralized, get organized! Take back the 20."[5] The image resembled a shooting range map of the United States where the bull's-eye was pointed at the twenty targeted districts.

On her Facebook page, which showed the map and featured the ad, Palin expressed the following:

With the president signing this *unwanted and "transformative" government takeover* of our health care system today with promises impossible to keep, let's not get discouraged. Don't get demoralized. Get organized!

We're going to reclaim the power of the people from those who disregarded the will of the people. We're going to fire them and send them back to the private sector, which has been shrinking thanks to their *destructive government-growing policies.* Maybe when they join the millions of unemployed, they'll understand why Americans wanted them to focus on job creation and an invigorated private sector. Come November, we're going to print pink slips for members of Congress as fast as they've been printing money.

We're paying particular attention to those House members who voted in favor of *Obamacare* and represent districts that Senator John McCain and I carried during the 2008 election. Three of these House members are retiring—from Arkansas's 2nd district, Indiana's 8th district, and Tennessee's 6th district—but we'll be working to make sure that those who replace them are Commonsense Conservatives. The others are running for re-election, and we're going to hold them accountable for this disastrous Obamacare vote. They are: Ann Kirkpatrick (AZ-1), Harry E. Mitchell (AZ-5), *Gabrielle Giffords* (AZ-8), John Salazar (CO-3), Betsy Markey (CO-4). Allen Boyd (FL-2), Suzanne M. Kosmas (FL-24), Baron P. Hill (IN-9), Earl Pomeroy (ND-AL),

158

Charlie Wilson (OH-6), John Boccieri (OH-16), Kathy Dahlkemper (PA-3), Christopher Carney (PA-10), John M. Spratt, Jr. (SC-5), Tom Perriello (VA-5), Alan B. Mollohan (WV-1), and Nick J. Rahall II (WV-3).

We'll aim for these races and many others. This is just the first salvo in a fight to elect people across the nation who will bring common sense to Washington. Please go to sarahpac.com and join me in the fight.

Stand tall, America. Real change is coming![6] (emphasis mine)

The Ugly Mouth constituents immediately came to the rescue to defend the much-criticized Sarah Palin and her so-called freedom of speech. Sarah Palin herself was silent. The following Monday, according to HuffPost Media, Rush Limbaugh spent his entire show undermining the media's political coverage of the Jared Loughner story.[7] Rush claimed the coverage was "childish and immature." Some excerpts from his show that Monday include the following, taken from Politicsdaily.com:

Reporters are bending over backwards to link this shooting to me, to Sarah Palin, to an entire industry—talk radio...Only in these instances is something said in the media, said to influence public behavior...All of this has been pure politics, disguised as compassion and concern for a congresswoman.[8]

I knew it was going to happen the minute I heard about the shooting...[It] was fatuous and silly to even verify and justify these accusations...The premise is insane, it's silly, it's beneath these people. Or is it? It is who they are.[9]

Rush Limbaugh lashed out with defensive comments for the majority of his Monday radio program, as noted by Huffingtonpost.com:

Even "the Obama government"—the FBI—calls Loughner a "deranged, insular irrational kid" who acted alone, Limbaugh

159

said. "The kid was evil. He was into the occult. He had an altar with a skull in his yard. Was God in his life? He was stalking the congresswoman."[10]

"The guy listened to heavy metal, and some of that anarchist stuff. We're dealing with an insane individual."[11]

"There is no evidence that he listened to talk radio. There is no evidence he listened to Fox News. There is no evidence that he saw Sarah Palin's Facebook page. No evidence he saw her lame website with the crosshairs."[12]

"Where are the parents? Are they derelicts? He was so devoted to marijuana he wanted to make it the new U.S. currency. Did anyone try to institutionalize him?"[13]

"This kid sounds like he was very well known as a dangerous element around town. If there is a file somewhere about this kid in the sheriff's office," said Rush, "and the sheriff had failed to act, then he would be partly responsible for the tragedy in Arizona on Saturday. If he was so concerned about the Tea Party, where was security for this congresswoman's event on Saturday?"[14]

"This Sheriff, Clarence Dupnik, is an anti-conservative."[15]

"Loughner is obviously deranged, so where's the left's safety net? Haven't we spent trillions of dollars to build a system to catch these disturbed people? Where is the evidence that their compassion works?"[16]

"It's not the right," Limbaugh said, "but the left that glorifies criminal behavior and violent imagery. 'No, no,' they say, 'that's art!' Rap music? 'That's art!'"[17]

They privately are thankful for Tucson because "they think it advances their sick and perverted purposes." Mark Penn, who was Bill Clinton's polltaker, said—before Tucson—that "Obama needs his own Oklahoma City."[18]

160

By linking Loughner to the right, Limbaugh warned, Democrats are "taking aim at a majority of the people in the country. This is not 1988, or 1993, when the drive-by media had total control. I am not going to be silenced," he said, but now he has too many allies. "They're accusing a majority of Americans of being accomplices to murder."[19]

"At no time has anybody ever called for violence," Limbaugh said. "We've never subtly promoted it." And, by the way, the Democrats' language is and was worse.[20]

Glenn Beck also defended Sarah Palin and her "crosshairs" advertisement. Mr. Beck reported on his radio broadcast the following Monday that he and Sarah Palin had discussed the shooting by e-mail. He read what he sent to Sarah on the air: "Sarah, as you know, peace is always the answer. I know you are feeling the same heat, if not much more on this. I want you to know you have my support. But please look into protection for your family. An attempt on you could bring the republic down." Beck continued, "There are nut-jobs on all sides...terror is terror. I don't care if it is for Allah or your party."[21]

Beck, who has made the claim on several occasions that President Obama wants him dead, also made the following comment regarding the Arizona shooting: "Sixty percent of Americans say the rhetoric in America has nothing to do with the shooting. It's—It's quite honestly an abomination that it's only 60 percent of the American people. I don't understand how rhetoric had anything to do with it. It's—there is zero evidence. And since when—since when had a spirited debate—I can be, and believe me I know I'm enemy number one of Barack Obama. Do I—do I think that he wants to kill me? He wants me dead."[22]

On January 12, Mrs. Palin broke her silence to express sympathy for the victims and respond to her critics. She released the following official statement:

Like millions of Americans I learned of the tragic events in Arizona on Saturday, and my heart broke for the innocent victims. No words can fill the hole left by the death of an innocent, but we do mourn for the victims' families as we express our sympathy.

I agree with the sentiments shared yesterday at the beautiful Catholic mass held in honor of the victims. The mass will hopefully help begin a healing process for the families touched by this tragedy and for our country.

Our exceptional nation, so vibrant with ideas and the passionate exchange and debate of ideas, is a light to the rest of the world. Congresswoman Giffords and her constituents were exercising their right to exchange ideas that day, to celebrate our Republic's core values and peacefully assemble to petition our government. It's inexcusable and incomprehensible why a single evil man took the lives of peaceful citizens that day.

There is a bittersweet irony that the strength of the American spirit shines brightest in times of tragedy. We saw that in Arizona. We saw the tenacity of those clinging to life, the compassion of those who kept the victims alive, and the heroism of those who overpowered a deranged gunman.

Like many, I've spent the past few days reflecting on what happened and praying for guidance. After this shocking tragedy, I listened at first puzzled, then with concern, and now with sadness, to the irresponsible statements from people attempting to apportion blame for this terrible event.

President Reagan said, "We must reject the idea that every time a law's broken, society is guilty rather than the lawbreaker. It is time to restore the American precept that each individual is accountable for his actions." Acts of monstrous criminality stand on their own. They begin and end with the criminals who commit them, not collectively with all the citizens of a state, not with those who listen to talk radio, not with maps of swing districts used by both sides of

The Ugly Mouths of America!

the aisle, not with law-abiding citizens who respectfully exercise their First Amendment rights at campaign rallies, not with those who proudly voted in the last election.

The last election was all about taking responsibility for our country's future. President Obama and I may not agree on everything, but I know he would join me in affirming the health of our democratic process. Two years ago his party was victorious. Last November, the other party won. In both elections the will of the American people was heard, and the peaceful transition of power proved yet again the enduring strength of our Republic.

Vigorous and spirited public debates during elections are among our most cherished traditions. And after the election, we shake hands and get back to work, and often both sides find common ground back in D.C. and elsewhere. If you don't like a person's vision for the country, you're free to debate that vision. If you don't like their ideas, you're free to propose better ideas. But, especially within hours of a tragedy unfolding, journalists and pundits should not manufacture a blood libel that serves only to incite the very hatred and violence they purport to condemn. That is reprehensible.

There are those who claim political rhetoric is to blame for the despicable act of this deranged, apparently apolitical criminal. And they claim political debate has somehow gotten more heated just recently. But when was it less heated? Back in those "calm days" when political figures literally settled their differences with dueling pistols? In an ideal world all discourse would be civil and all disagreements cordial. But our Founding Fathers knew they weren't designing a system for perfect men and women. If men and women were angels, there would be no need for government. Our Founders' genius was to design a system that helped settle the inevitable conflicts caused by our imperfect passions in civil ways. So, we must condemn violence if our Republic is to endure.

As I said while campaigning for others last March in Arizona during a very heated primary race, "We know violence isn't the answer. When we 'take up our arms', we're talking about our vote." Yes, our debates are full of passion, but we settle our political differences respectfully at the ballot box—as we did just two months ago, and as our Republic enables us to do again in the next election, and the next. That's who we are as Americans and how we were meant to be. Public discourse and debate isn't a sign of crisis, but of our enduring strength. It is part of why America is exceptional.

No one should be deterred from speaking up and speaking out in peaceful dissent, and we certainly must not be deterred by those who embrace evil and call it good. And we will not be stopped from celebrating the greatness of our country and our foundational freedoms by those who mock its greatness by being intolerant of differing opinion and seeking to muzzle dissent with shrill cries of imagined insults.

Just days before she was shot, Congresswoman Giffords read the First Amendment on the floor of the House. It was a beautiful moment and more than simply "symbolic," as some claim, to have the Constitution read by our Congress. I am confident she knew that reading our sacred charter of liberty was more than just "symbolic." But less than a week after Congresswoman Giffords reaffirmed our protected freedoms, another member of Congress announced that he would propose a law that would criminalize speech he found offensive.

It is in the hour when our values are challenged that we must remain resolved to protect those values. Recall how the events of 9-11 challenged our values and we had to fight the tendency to trade our freedoms for perceived security. And so it is today.

Let us honor those precious lives cut short in Tucson by praying for them and their families and by cherishing their memories. Let us pray for the full recovery of the wounded. And let us pray for our country. In times like this we need
164

God's guidance and the peace He provides. We need strength to not let the random acts of a criminal turn us against ourselves, or weaken our solid foundation, or provide a pretext to stifle debate.

America must be stronger than the evil we saw displayed last week. We are better than the mindless finger-pointing we endured in the wake of the tragedy. We will come out of this stronger and more united in our desire to peacefully engage in the great debates of our time, to respectfully embrace our differences in a positive manner, and to unite in the knowledge that, though our ideas may be different, we must all strive for a better future for our country. May God bless America.[23]

We may never know whether Palin's "crosshairs" map or the comments she'd made to audiences of thousands—such as "don't retreat, reload"—inspired Jared Lee Loughner's deranged shooting attack. But the very fact that this kind of political rhetoric is in question should indicate to us the divisive effect it has on the public. This abusive use of our freedom of speech is dangerous. As Mrs. Palin put it, it may be "vigorous and spirited," but not everyone shakes hands and makes all well once the election is over. In fact, some only express more anger and are spiritually motivated by the controversial speech coming from the daily broadcasts of the Ugly Mouths to become more vigorous and perhaps more aggressive. Listening to or viewing such programs, like anything else, can become habitual. As Sheriff Dupnick so clearly stated, "The anger, the hatred, the bigotry that goes on in this country is getting to be outrageous, and it's not without consequences."

The wounded victim, Gabrielle "Gabby" Giffords, is the wife of American astronaut Mark E. Kelly, part of the team for the space shuttle Endeavor. Mark prayerfully remained at her bedside for the days after the shooting, watching his wife struggle for survival while in a medical-induced coma.

165

Four days after the shooting, on January 12, 2011, President Obama and his wife Michelle visited Congresswoman Giffords in the hospital. After the president had left the hospital room, Mark asked his wife to give him a thumbs-up if she could see the president. Gabby raised her arm ever so slightly in response. Shortly thereafter, President Obama was scheduled to be the closing speaker at a memorial service for the victims of that deadly shooting. Devoting a significant portion of his remarks to the memory of the victims, President Obama announced on national TV and to the world, to a loud melodious applause, that Gabby had opened her eyes for the first time after the deadly shooting. The president said, "She knows we're here, and she knows we love her." As this joyous announcement was being made, First Lady Michelle Obama held hands with Gabby's husband, Mark. Mr. Obama continued, "I believe we can be better...Those who died here, those who saved lives here—they help me believe. We may not be able to stop all evil in the world, but I know that how we treat one another is entirely up to us."[24]

The president did acknowledge that there was no sure way of knowing what had truly motivated the shooting and who really was to blame. Instead he said, "At a time when our discourse has become so sharply polarized, at a time when we are far too eager to lay the blame for all that ails the world at the feet of those who think differently than we do, it's important for us to pause for a moment and make sure that we are talking with each other in a way that heals, not a way that wounds."[25]

I truly, whole-heartedly agree with these words. We all have the right of free speech; therefore, each of us has the right to express his or her opinion. But the way an opinion is delivered should be respectful and considerate for those who may or may not share your viewpoint. This is the main problem with the UMAs. They seem to have the attitude and spiritual belief that they have the right to infringe on everyone else's rights by expressing themselves with offensive speech. This is wrong.

166

The recovery progress that Gabrielle Giffords has made since the shooting has been clear, very definable, and simply miraculous. In the words of Dr. Michael Lemole, "We're wise to acknowledge miracles."[26] It is a testimony to the power of prayer, faith, scientific know-how, and medical advancement.

In May, just three and a half months after the shooting, Gabby visited the Kennedy Space Center in Florida and watched the space shuttle Endeavour lift off with her husband Mark aboard.

In June, after her husband's return to Earth, Gabby was released from the hospital and went home to League City, Texas. There, she continued to receive round-the-clock assistance.

In August, Gabby returned to Capitol Hill to participate in the momentous vote on the nation's debt ceiling. She received a standing ovation from the crowd of her colleagues. Her presence alone and the simple acts of walking, smiling, and greeting others by giving and receiving hugs proved her remarkable strength and recovery. She voted in favor of the bill, which passed 269 to 161.

On January 24, 2012, Gabby made the announcement that she would not return to run for reelection to public office. Instead, she said, she and her family would focus on her recovery. That same day, at the opening of the State of the Union address, she was given a warm and timely hug by the president to the applause and standing ovation of the full house of both Democrats and Republicans. For Gabby and her family, there is no doubt that there is so much more work to do on the road to her medical and physical recovery. A career in politics is very stressful, and although she will be missed by so many, we all understand. For certain, her spirit is strong, her mind is determined, and her body is willing. For our part, may a multitude of heartfelt prayers continue to go up on behalf of Gabby Giffords

Chapter 9: Outside In, the Conclusion

I named the final section of this publication *Outside In* because I wanted to reflect on the message and purpose of this book. For the vast majority of us, we stand on the outside listening and looking in. It's not that we aren't pro-American, or a U.S. citizen, or greatly concerned about the news of the day, rather we are not part of the inner circle of government, or the main stream media that have the responsibility of reporting. So basically, we stand (or sit) on the outside, reading the paper, watching the news, searching the Internet, or listening to the radio which helps us to form an opinion of a current event.

As I stated in the introduction, I am originally from Chicago, Illinois. I am not highly educated, but have worked all my adult life and earned a good living. In other words, I am your "average Joe". I too stand on the outside. My writing was entirely the result of listening, observing, and researching; so that I have become the reporter or the journalist.

In reality, how do any of us really know the truth of a news event or the accusation of the underhanded activity of government? Unless we were actually there and observed or witnessed in detail the event, we are on the outside tuning in to learn what's happening. We depend on the reporters or commentators, the ones on the inside to gather detailed information and accurately share it with us.

Included among the inside ones are the ugly mouths. They share the information or the event of the day with their opinionated propaganda in order to sway our thinking on a particular subject. This is not an uncommon practice. Whether we recognize it or not, we are bombarded with commercials, billboards, Internet pop ups, and other forms of advertisements all day and every day. But the problem with the UMAs is the stealth-like delivery and the hatefulness of their messages.

Our nation is facing many challenges abroad and within our own borders. Economist, journalist, scientist, and

168

politicians agree that we are at a pivotal time in US history. In addition, our society is composed of a melting pot of different cultures and ethical backgrounds. All of "the people", collectively as an organization, or individually, we have our own attitudes, perceptions, beliefs, trusts, practices, and teachings. This greatly emphasizes the responsible need to promote unity, respect, appreciation, and concern for one another. But I fear that the Ugly Mouths of America contradict that responsibility.

There is a way to disagree without becoming disagreeable. To disagree one expresses a different opinion. We all have opinions, and they do not always agree, and this is fine. But the UMAs are often disagreeable; this denotes an unpleasant, bad-tempered, obnoxious, and offensive way to express an opinion. The problem with being disagreeable is that it teaches disrespect of others. The UMA places himself or herself in the position of 'absolute correctness' and the opposing opinions are demoralized and ridiculed.

The underlying spirit of me-ism or the 'all important me' displayed in the UMAs communication has a crippling effect on society. It promotes the pander that it's ok to be rude or disrespectful. It tells its audience, "name calling is acceptable", "to hate others that do not agree with you is fine", it's the norm, "if they are different from you, then something is wrong with them".

After observing the UMAs for the past several years, I found their programs can easily become addictive. At certain times of the day, you say to yourself, "I wonder what this one or that one is going to talk about today?" Sometimes their message can be a bit humorous, even entertaining, but often it was annoying and stirred the emotions of anger and resentment. Why anger? It was because their message often had underlying racial innuendos, or in the case of Neal Boortz, outspoken racial slurs. Resentment was due primarily to the fact that there was no fair opportunity to respond to their message or comment. One might ask, "If it makes you feel that way, why don't their audience just change the channel, or turn it off?" The answer is simple, you develop a curious desire to see or hear, 'what are they

169

going to say next, or just how are they going to spend this one?' The underlying danger is that when you listen to something everyday, you tend to remember it. Knowingly or unknowingly, you gradually find yourself adopting its views and opinions.

The effect of viewing or listening to something everyday, and in some cases all day, is evident in marketing and advertising. This is what causes people to purchase a certain product, or trust a particular brand. Buy watching or listening to the UMAs constantly, we began to trust them, believe in them, and often imitate their demeanor. As a result, we began to think differently, we develop the same "spirit". It changes us and we change society.

Let's be real—why are the ugly mouths so popular? It's because of the same reasons reality TV has taken over television. American's have an insatiable desire for drama and controversy. Stretching the boundaries and fueling the fire has become big business with big opportunities. Like a reality TV personality, the UMAs need to drive conflict and controversy to make money. To disagree in a civil manner does not draw the audience they need to be successful. To attempt to have an intelligent, civilized conversation, focused on the facts and issues would be like a drug addict trying to go cold turkey. It's possible, it can be done, but it's not easily accomplished.

UMA's like the easy route of stirring controversy and making money. They appear to promote patriotism, but actually they are promoting their opinion of what's American. This may include political choices, their concept of laws, support for organizations, dislike of unions, or racial tension. Combining jingoism with the story of the day, they decipher the news, mix in the controversy and throw it against the wall to see what sticks.

The advertisers or sponsors of the UMA's programs have found this avenue of marketing to be an effective way to reach the consumer. Not only do they connect with the basic senses of sight and hearing, but they enhance their advertisements with the emotions of fear, anger, resentment, and outrage.

The poignant reality is that this trend of marketing is growing. The concept is not how you get the audience to listen, but simply draw in the audience and we will turn them into consumers, political support, or organizational members. The ugly mouth masters, those who make millions of dollars with propaganda schemes of this sort, are major contributors whether they knowing acknowledge their culpability or not.

This book is not about the abandonment of hope or the right to have an opposing opinion, but rather a call to action for the audience to resist the manipulation of the UMAs and take their words for what they really are— opinions. They're selling the hype and controversy—without it, they do not make their millions.

.

The Ugly Mouths of America!

"I Have a Dream"

Martin Luther King Jr. - Address in Washington D.C.,

August 28th, 1963

Transcript from AmericianRhetoric.com

"I am happy to join with you today in what will go down in history as the greatest demonstration for freedom in the history of our nation.

Five score years ago, a great American, in whose symbolic shadow we stand signed the Emancipation Proclamation. This momentous decree came as a great beacon light of hope to millions of Negro slaves who had been seared in the flames of withering injustice. It came as a joyous daybreak to end the long night of captivity.

But one hundred years later, we must face the tragic fact that the Negro is still not free. One hundred years later, the life of the Negro is still sadly crippled by the manacles of segregation and the chains of discrimination. One hundred years later, the Negro lives on a lonely island of poverty in the midst of a vast ocean of material prosperity. One hundred years later, the Negro is still languishing in the corners of American society and finds himself an exile in his own land. So we have come here today to dramatize an shameful condition.

In a sense we have come to our nation's capital to cash a check. When the architects of our republic wrote the magnificent words of the Constitution and the Declaration of Independence, they were signing a promissory note to which every American was to fall heir. This note was a promise that all men, yes black men as well as white men, would be guaranteed the unalienable rights of "life, liberty and the pursuit of happiness". It is obvious today that America has defaulted on this promissory note, insofar as her citizens of color are concerned. Instead of honoring this sacred obligation, America has given the Negro people a bad check,

The Ugly Mouths of America!

a check which has come back marked "insufficient funds."

But we refuse to believe that the bank of justice is bankrupt. We refuse to believe that there are insufficient funds in the great vaults of opportunity of this nation. And so, we come to cash this check, a check that will give us upon demand the riches of freedom and the security of justice.

We have also come to this hallowed spot to remind America of the fierce urgency of now. This is no time to engage in the luxury of cooling off or to take the tranquilizing drug of gradualism. Now is the time to make real the promises of democracy. Now is the time to rise from the dark and desolate valley of segregation to the sunlit path of racial justice. Now is the time to lift our nation from the quicksand of racial injustice to the solid rock of brotherhood. Now is the time to make justice a reality for all of God's children.

It will be fatal for the nation to overlook the urgency of the moment. This sweltering summer of the Negro's legitimate discontent will not pass until there is an invigorating autumn of freedom and equality. Nineteen sixty-three is not an end, but a beginning. And those who hope that the Negro needed to blow of steam and will now be content will have a rude awakening if the nation returns to business as usual. And there will be neither rest nor tranquility in America until the Negro is granted his citizenships rights. The whirlwinds of revolt will continue to shake the foundations of our nation until the bright day of justice emerges.

But there is something that I must say to my people, who stand on the warm threshold which leads into the palace of justice: In the process of gaining our rightful place, we must not be guilty of wrongful deeds. Let us not seek to satisfy our thirst for freedom by drinking from the cup of bitterness and hatred. We must forever conduct our struggle on the high plane of dignity and discipline. We must not allow our creative protest to degenerate into physical violence. Again and again, we must rise to the majestic heights of meeting physical force with soul force.

The Ugly Mouths of America!

The marvelous new militancy which has engulfed the Negro community must not lead us to a distrust of all white people, for many of our white brothers, as evidenced by their presence here today, have come to realize that their destiny is tied up with our destiny. And they have come to realize that their freedom is inextricably bound to our freedom.

We cannot walk alone. And as we walk, we must make the pledge that we shall always march ahead. We cannot turn back.

There are those who are asking the devotees of civil rights, "When will you be satisfied?" We can never be satisfied as long as the Negro is the victim of the unspeakable horrors of police brutality. We can never be satisfied as long as our bodies, heavy with the fatigue of travel, cannot gain lodging in the motels of the highways and the hotels of the cities. We cannot be satisfied as long as the Negro's basic mobility is from a smaller ghetto to a larger one. We can never be satisfied as long as our children are stripped of their self-hood and robbed of their dignity by signs stating: "For Whites Only." We cannot be satisfied as long as a Negro in Mississippi cannot vote and a Negro in New York believes he has nothing for which to vote. No, no, we are not satisfied, and we will not be satisfied until "justice rolls down like waters, and righteousness like a mighty stream."

I am not unmindful that some of you have come here out of great trials and tribulations. Some of you have come fresh from narrow jail cells. And some of you have come from areas where your quest -- quest for freedom left you battered by the storms of persecution and staggered by the winds of police brutality. You have been the veterans of creative suffering. Continue to work with the faith that unearned suffering is redemptive. Go back to Mississippi, go back to Alabama, go back to South Carolina, go back to Georgia, go back to Louisiana, go back to the slums and ghettos of our northern cities, knowing that somehow this situation can and will be changed.

The Ugly Mouths of America!

Let us not wallow in the valley of despair, I say to you today, my friends, that in spite of the difficulties and frustrations of the moment, I still have a dream. It is a dream deeply rooted in the American dream.

I have a dream that one day this nation will rise up and live out the true meaning of its creed:" We hold these truths to be self-evident: that all men are created equal."

I have a dream that one day on the red hills of Georgia the sons of former slaves and the sons of former slave owners will be able to sit down together at a table of brotherhood.

I have a dream that one day even the state of Mississippi, a desert state, sweltering with the heat of injustice and oppression, will be transformed into as oasis of freedom and justice.

I have a dream that my four children will one day live in a nation where they will not be judged by the color of their skin but by the content of their character.

I have a dream today.

I have a dream that one day the state of Alabama, whose governor's lips are presently dripping with the words of interposition and nullification, will be transformed into a situation where little black boys and black girls will be able to join hands with little white boys and white girls and walk together as sisters and brothers.

I have a dream today.

I have a dream that one day every valley shall be exalted, every hill and mountain shall be made low, the rough places will be made plain, and the crooked places will be made straight, and the glory of the Lord shall be revealed, and all flesh shall see it together.

This is our hope. This is the faith with which I return to the South. With this faith we will be able to hew out of the mountain of despair a stone of hope. With this faith we will be able to transform the jingling discords of our nation into a

The Ugly Mouths of America!

beautiful symphony of brotherhood. With this faith we will be able to work together, to pray together, to struggle together, to stand up for freedom together, knowing that we will be free one day.

This will be the day when all of God's children will be able to sing with a new meaning, "My country, 'tis of thee, sweet land of liberty, of thee I sing. Land where my fathers died, land of the pilgrim's pride, from every mountainside, let freedom ring.

And id America is to be a great nation, this must become true.

And so let freedom ring from the prodigious hilltops of New Hampshire. Let freedom ring from the mighty mountains of New York. Let freedom ring from the heightening Alleghenies of Pennsylvania. Let freedom ring from the snow-capped Rockies of Colorado. Let freedom ring from the curvaceous slopes of California.

But not only that: Let freedom ring from Stone Mountain Georgia. Let freedom ring from Lookout Mountain of Tennessee. Let freedom ring from every hill and molehill of Mississippi. From every mountainside, let freedom ring.

*And when this happens, when we allow freedom ring, when we let it ring from every village and every hamlet, from every state and every city, we will be able to speed up that day when all of God's children, black men and white men, Jews and Gentiles, Protestants and Catholics, will be able to join hands and sing the words of the old Negro spiritual, "Free at last! Free at last! **Thank God Almighty, we are free at last**!"*

★ ★ ★ ★ ★ ★ ★ ★ ★ ★

The Ugly Mouths of America!

Obama's Victory Speech

November 4th, 2008 - Chicago, Illinois

Transcription by www.America.gov

PRESIDENT-ELECT BARACK OBAMA: *Hello, Chicago.*

If there is anyone out there who still doubts that America is a place where all things are possible, who still wonders if the dream of our founders is alive in our time, who still questions the power of our democracy, tonight is your answer.

It's the answer told by lines that stretched around schools and churches in numbers this nation has never seen, by people who waited three hours and four hours, many for the first time in their lives, because they believed that this time must be different, that their voices could be that difference.

It's the answer spoken by young and old, rich and poor, Democrat and Republican, black, white, Hispanic, Asian, Native American, gay, straight, disabled and not disabled. Americans who sent a message to the world that we have never been just a collection of individuals or a collection of red states and blue states.

We are, and always will be, the United States of America.

It's the answer that led those who've been told for so long by so many to be cynical and fearful and doubtful about what we can achieve to put their hands on the arc of history and bend it once more toward the hope of a better day.

It's been a long time coming, but tonight, because of what we did on this date, in this election, at this defining moment, change has come to America.

A little bit earlier this evening, I received an extraordinarily gracious call from Sen. McCain.

Sen. McCain fought long and hard in this campaign. And he's fought even longer and harder for the country that he loves. He has endured sacrifices for America that most of us cannot begin to imagine. We are better off for the service rendered by this brave and selfless leader.

I congratulate him; I congratulate Gov. Palin for all that they've achieved. And I look forward to working with them to renew this nation's promise in the months ahead.

I want to thank my partner in this journey, a man who campaigned from his heart, and spoke for the men and women he grew up with on the streets of Scranton and rode with on the train home to Delaware, the vice president-elect of the United States, Joe Biden.

And I would not be standing here tonight without the unyielding support of my best friend for the last 16 years, the rock of our family, the love of my life, the nation's next first lady, Michelle Obama.

Sasha and Malia, I love you both more than you can imagine. And you have earned the new puppy that's coming with us to the new White House.

And while she's no longer with us, I know my grandmother's watching, along with the family that made me who I am. I miss them tonight. I know that my debt to them is beyond measure.

To my sister Maya, my sister Alma, all my other brothers and sisters, thank you so much for all the support that you've given me. I am grateful to them.

And to my campaign manager, David Plouffe, the unsung hero of this campaign, who built the best — the best political campaign, I think, in the history of the United States of America.

To my chief strategist David Axelrod who's been a partner with me every step of the way.

178

To the best campaign team ever assembled in the history of politics. You made this happen, and I am forever grateful for what you've sacrificed to get it done.

But above all, I will never forget who this victory truly belongs to. It belongs to you. It belongs to you.

I was never the likeliest candidate for this office. We didn't start with much money or many endorsements. Our campaign was not hatched in the halls of Washington. It began in the backyards of Des Moines and the living rooms of Concord and the front porches of Charleston. It was built by working men and women who dug into what little savings they had to give $5 and $10 and $20 to the cause.

It grew strength from the young people who rejected the myth of their generation's apathy, who left their homes and their families for jobs that offered little pay and less sleep.

It drew strength from the not-so-young people who braved the bitter cold and scorching heat to knock on doors of perfect strangers, and from the millions of Americans who volunteered and organized and proved that more than two centuries later a government of the people, by the people, and for the people has not perished from the Earth.

This is your victory.

And I know you didn't do this just to win an election. And I know you didn't do it for me.

You did it because you understand the enormity of the task that lies ahead. For even as we celebrate tonight, we know the challenges that tomorrow will bring are the greatest of our lifetime — two wars, a planet in peril, the worst financial crisis in a century.

Even as we stand here tonight, we know there are brave Americans waking up in the deserts of Iraq and the mountains of Afghanistan to risk their lives for us.

There are mothers and fathers who will lie awake after the children fall asleep and wonder how they'll make the

179

mortgage or pay their doctors' bills or save enough for their child's college education.

There's new energy to harness, new jobs to be created, new schools to build, and threats to meet, alliances to repair.

The road ahead will be long. Our climb will be steep. We may not get there in one year or even in one term. But, America, I have never been more hopeful than I am tonight that we will get there.

I promise you, we as a people will get there.

There will be setbacks and false starts. There are many who won't agree with every decision or policy I make as president. And we know the government can't solve every problem.

But I will always be honest with you about the challenges we face. I will listen to you, especially when we disagree. And, above all, I will ask you to join in the work of remaking this nation, the only way it's been done in America for 221 years — block by block, brick by brick, calloused hand by calloused hand.

What began 21 months ago in the depths of winter cannot end on this autumn night.

This victory alone is not the change we seek. It is only the chance for us to make that change. And that cannot happen if we go back to the way things were.

It can't happen without you, without a new spirit of service, a new spirit of sacrifice.

So let us summon a new spirit of patriotism, of responsibility, where each of us resolves to pitch in and work harder and look after not only ourselves but each other.

Let us remember that, if this financial crisis taught us anything, it's that we cannot have a thriving Wall Street while Main Street suffers.

The Ugly Mouths of America!

In this country, we rise or fall as one nation, as one people. Let's resist the temptation to fall back on the same partisanship and pettiness and immaturity that has poisoned our politics for so long.

Let's remember that it was a man from this state who first carried the banner of the Republican Party to the White House, a party founded on the values of self-reliance and individual liberty and national unity.

Those are values that we all share. And while the Democratic Party has won a great victory tonight, we do so with a measure of humility and determination to heal the divides that have held back our progress.

As Lincoln said to a nation far more divided than ours, we are not enemies but friends. Though passion may have strained, it must not break our bonds of affection.

And to those Americans whose support I have yet to earn, I may not have won your vote tonight, but I hear your voices. I need your help. And I will be your president, too.

And to all those watching tonight from beyond our shores, from parliaments and palaces, to those who are huddled around radios in the forgotten corners of the world: Our stories are singular, but our destiny is shared, and a new dawn of American leadership is at hand.

To those — to those who would tear the world down: We will defeat you. To those who seek peace and security: We support you. And to all those who have wondered if America's beacon still burns as bright: Tonight we proved once more that the true strength of our nation comes not from the might of our arms or the scale of our wealth, but from the enduring power of our ideals: democracy, liberty, opportunity and unyielding hope.

That's the true genius of America: that America can change. Our union can be perfected. What we've already achieved gives us hope for what we can and must achieve tomorrow.

The Ugly Mouths of America!

This election had many firsts and many stories that will be told for generations. But one that's on my mind tonight's about a woman who cast her ballot in Atlanta. She's a lot like the millions of others who stood in line to make their voice heard in this election except for one thing: Ann Nixon Cooper is 106 years old.

She was born just a generation past slavery; a time when there were no cars on the road or planes in the sky; when someone like her couldn't vote for two reasons — because she was a woman and because of the color of her skin.

And tonight, I think about all that she's seen throughout her century in America — the heartache and the hope; the struggle and the progress; the times we were told that we can't, and the people who pressed on with that American creed: Yes we can.

At a time when women's voices were silenced and their hopes dismissed, she lived to see them stand up and speak out and reach for the ballot. Yes we can.

When there was despair in the dust bowl and depression across the land, she saw a nation conquer fear itself with a New Deal, new jobs, a new sense of common purpose. Yes we can.

When the bombs fell on our harbor and tyranny threatened the world, she was there to witness a generation rise to greatness and a democracy was saved. Yes we can.

She was there for the buses in Montgomery, the hoses in Birmingham, a bridge in Selma, and a preacher from Atlanta who told a people that "We Shall Overcome." Yes we can.

A man touched down on the moon, a wall came down in Berlin, a world was connected by our own science and imagination.

And this year, in this election, she touched her finger to a screen, and cast her vote, because after 106 years in

The Ugly Mouths of America!

America, through the best of times and the darkest of hours, she knows how America can change.

Yes we can.

America, we have come so far. We have seen so much. But there is so much more to do. So tonight, let us ask ourselves — if our children should live to see the next century; if my daughters should be so lucky to live as long as Ann Nixon Cooper, what change will they see? What progress will we have made?

This is our chance to answer that call. This is our moment.

This is our time, to put our people back to work and open doors of opportunity for our kids; to restore prosperity and promote the cause of peace; to reclaim the American dream and reaffirm that fundamental truth, that, out of many, we are one; that while we breathe, we hope. And where we are met with cynicism and doubts and those who tell us that we can't, we will respond with that timeless creed that sums up the spirit of a people: Yes, we can.

Thank you. God bless you. And may God bless the United States of America.

The Ugly Mouths of America!

Obama's Inauguration Address

January, 20, 2009

Transcription by CQ Transcriptions:

PRESIDENT BARACK OBAMA: *Thank you. Thank you.*

My fellow citizens: I stand here today humbled by the task before us, grateful for the trust you have bestowed, mindful of the sacrifices borne by our ancestors.

I thank President Bush for his service to our nation... as well as the generosity and cooperation he has shown throughout this transition.

Forty-four Americans have now taken the presidential oath.

The words have been spoken during rising tides of prosperity and the still waters of peace. Yet, every so often the oath is taken amidst gathering clouds and raging storms. At these moments, America has carried on not simply because of the skill or vision of those in high office, but because We the People have remained faithful to the ideals of our forebears, and true to our founding documents.

So it has been. So it must be with this generation of Americans.

That we are in the midst of crisis is now well understood. Our nation is at war against a far-reaching network of violence and hatred. Our economy is badly weakened, a consequence of greed and irresponsibility on the part of some but also our collective failure to make hard choices and prepare the nation for a new age.

Homes have been lost, jobs shed, businesses shuttered. Our health care is too costly, our schools fail too many, and each day brings further evidence that the ways we use energy strengthen our adversaries and threaten our planet.

These are the indicators of crisis, subject to data and statistics. Less measurable, but no less profound, is a sapping of confidence across our land; a nagging fear that America's decline is inevitable, that the next generation must lower its sights.

Today I say to you that the challenges we face are real, they are serious and they are many. They will not be met easily or in a short span of time. But know this America: They will be met.

On this day, we gather because we have chosen hope over fear, unity of purpose over conflict and discord.

On this day, we come to proclaim an end to the petty grievances and false promises, the recriminations and worn-out dogmas that for far too long have strangled our politics.

We remain a young nation, but in the words of Scripture, the time has come to set aside childish things. The time has come to reaffirm our enduring spirit; to choose our better history; to carry forward that precious gift, that noble idea, passed on from generation to generation: the God-given promise that all are equal, all are free, and all deserve a chance to pursue their full measure of happiness.

In reaffirming the greatness of our nation, we understand that greatness is never a given. It must be earned. Our journey has never been one of shortcuts or settling for less.

It has not been the path for the faint-hearted, for those who prefer leisure over work, or seek only the pleasures of riches and fame.

185

Rather, it has been the risk-takers, the doers, the makers of things -- some celebrated, but more often men and women obscure in their labor -- who have carried us up the long, rugged path towards prosperity and freedom.

For us, they packed up their few worldly possessions and traveled across oceans in search of a new life. For us, they toiled in sweatshops and settled the West, endured the lash of the whip and plowed the hard earth.

For us, they fought and died in places Concord and Gettysburg; Normandy and Khe Sanh.

Time and again these men and women struggled and sacrificed and worked till their hands were raw so that we might live a better life. They saw America as bigger than the sum of our individual ambitions; greater than all the differences of birth or wealth or faction.

This is the journey we continue today. We remain the most prosperous, powerful nation on Earth. Our workers are no less productive than when this crisis began. Our minds are no less inventive, our goods and services no less needed than they were last week or last month or last year. Our capacity remains undiminished. But our time of standing pat, of protecting narrow interests and putting off unpleasant decisions -- that time has surely passed.

Starting today, we must pick ourselves up, dust ourselves off, and begin again the work of remaking AmericaFor everywhere we look, there is work to be done.

The state of our economy calls for action: bold and swift. And we will act not only to create new jobs but to lay a new foundation for growth.

We will build the roads and bridges, the electric grids and digital lines that feed our commerce and bind us together.

The Ugly Mouths of America!

We will restore science to its rightful place and wield technology's wonders to raise health care's quality... and lower its costs.

We will harness the sun and the winds and the soil to fuel our cars and run our factories. And we will transform our schools and colleges and universities to meet the demands of a new age.

All this we can do. All this we will do.

Now, there are some who question the scale of our ambitions, who suggest that our system cannot tolerate too many big plans. Their memories are short, for they have forgotten what this country has already done, what free men and women can achieve when imagination is joined to common purpose and necessity to courage.

What the cynics fail to understand is that the ground has shifted beneath them, that the stale political arguments that have consumed us for so long, no longer apply.

MR. The question we ask today is not whether our government is too big or too small, but whether it works, whether it helps families find jobs at a decent wage, care they can afford, a retirement that is dignified.

Where the answer is yes, we intend to move forward. Where the answer is no, programs will end.

And those of us who manage the public's dollars will be held to account, to spend wisely, reform bad habits, and do our business in the light of day, because only then can we restore the vital trust between a people and their government.

Nor is the question before us whether the market is a force for good or ill. Its power to generate wealth and expand freedom is unmatched.

The Ugly Mouths of America!

But this crisis has reminded us that without a watchful eye, the market can spin out of control. The nation cannot prosper long when it favors only the prosperous.

The success of our economy has always depended not just on the size of our gross domestic product, but on the reach of our prosperity; on the ability to extend opportunity to every willing heart -- not out of charity, but because it is the surest route to our common good

As for our common defense, we reject as false the choice between our safety and our ideals.

Our founding fathers faced with perils that we can scarcely imagine, drafted a charter to assure the rule of law and the rights of man, a charter expanded by the blood of generations.

Those ideals still light the world, and we will not give them up for expedience's sake.

And so, to all other peoples and governments who are watching today, from the grandest capitals to the small village where my father was born: know that America is a friend of each nation and every man, woman and child who seeks a future of peace and dignity, and we are ready to lead once more.

Recall that earlier generations faced down fascism and communism not just with missiles and tanks, but with the sturdy alliances and enduring convictions.

They understood that our power alone cannot protect us, nor does it entitle us to do as we please. Instead, they knew that our power grows through its prudent use. Our security emanates from the justness of our cause; the force of our example; the tempering qualities of humility and restraint.

We are the keepers of this legacy, guided by these principles once more, we can meet those new threats that demand

188

even greater effort, even greater cooperation and understanding between nations. We'll begin to responsibly leave Iraq to its people and forge a hard- earned peace in Afghanistan.

With old friends and former foes, we'll work tirelessly to lessen the nuclear threat and roll back the specter of a warming planet.

We will not apologize for our way of life nor will we waver in its defense.

And for those who seek to advance their aims by inducing terror and slaughtering innocents, we say to you now that, "Our spirit is stronger and cannot be broken. You cannot outlast us, and we will defeat you."

For we know that our patchwork heritage is a strength, not a weakness.

We are a nation of Christians and Muslims, Jews and Hindus, and nonbelievers. We are shaped by every language and culture, drawn from every end of this Earth.

And because we have tasted the bitter swill of civil war and segregation and emerged from that dark chapter stronger and more united, we cannot help but believe that the old hatreds shall someday pass; that the lines of tribe shall soon dissolve; that as the world grows smaller, our common humanity shall reveal itself; and that America must play its role in ushering in a new era of peace.

To the Muslim world, we seek a new way forward, based on mutual interest and mutual respect.

To those leaders around the globe who seek to sow conflict or blame their society's ills on the West, know that your people will judge you on what you can build, not what you destroy.

The Ugly Mouths of America!

To those.. To those who cling to power through corruption and deceit and the silencing of dissent, know that you are on the wrong side of history, but that we will extend a hand if you are willing to unclench your fist.

To the people of poor nations, we pledge to work alongside you to make your farms flourish and let clean waters flow; to nourish starved bodies and feed hungry minds.

And to those nations like ours that enjoy relative plenty, we say we can no longer afford indifference to the suffering outside our borders, nor can we consume the world's resources without regard to effect. For the world has changed, and we must change with it.

As we consider the road that unfolds before us, we remember with humble gratitude those brave Americans who, at this very hour, patrol far-off deserts and distant mountains. They have something to tell us, just as the fallen heroes who lie in Arlington whisper through the ages.

We honor them not only because they are guardians of our liberty, but because they embody the spirit of service: a willingness to find meaning in something greater than themselves.

And yet, at this moment, a moment that will define a generation, it is precisely this spirit that must inhabit us all.

For as much as government can do and must do, it is ultimately the faith and determination of the American people upon which this nation relies.

It is the kindness to take in a stranger when the levees break; the selflessness of workers who would rather cut their hours than see a friend lose their job which sees us through our darkest hours.

190

It is the firefighter's courage to storm a stairway filled with smoke, but also a parent's willingness to nurture a child, that finally decides our fate.

Our challenges may be new, the instruments with which we meet them may be new, but those values upon which our success depends, honesty and hard work, courage and fair play, tolerance and curiosity, loyalty and patriotism -- these things are old.

These things are true. They have been the quiet force of progress throughout our history.

What is demanded then is a return to these truths. What is required of us now is a new era of responsibility -- a recognition, on the part of every American, that we have duties to ourselves, our nation and the world, duties that we do not grudgingly accept but rather seize gladly, firm in the knowledge that there is nothing so satisfying to the spirit, so defining of our character than giving our all to a difficult task.

This is the price and the promise of citizenship.

This is the source of our confidence: the knowledge that God calls on us to shape an uncertain destiny.

This is the meaning of our liberty and our creed, why men and women and children of every race and every faith can join in celebration across this magnificent mall. And why a man whose father less than 60 years ago might not have been served at a local restaurant can now stand before you to take a most sacred oath.

So let us mark this day in remembrance of who we are and how far we have traveled.

In the year of America's birth, in the coldest of months, a small band of patriots huddled by dying campfires on the shores of an icy river.

191

The capital was abandoned. The enemy was advancing. The snow was stained with blood.

At a moment when the outcome of our revolution was most in doubt, the father of our nation ordered these words be read to the people:

"Let it be told to the future world that in the depth of winter, when nothing but hope and virtue could survive, that the city and the country, alarmed at one common danger, came forth to meet it."

America, in the face of our common dangers, in this winter of our hardship, let us remember these timeless words; with hope and virtue, let us brave once more the icy currents, and endure what storms may come; let it be said by our children's children that when we were tested we refused to let this journey end, that we did not turn back nor did we falter; and with eyes fixed on the horizon and God's grace upon us, we carried forth that great gift of freedom and delivered it safely to future generations.

Thank you. God bless you. And God bless the United States of America.

The Ugly Mouths of America!

Authors Notes

Introduction- An Ugly Mouth!

[1]*The Washington Post, Limbaugh Audience Size? It's Largely Up in the Air, Paul Farhi, Washington Post Staff writer, March 7, 2009*

[2]*Media Matters of America, June 26, 2009; from the June 26 edition of Premier Radio Networks' The Rush Limbaugh Show.*

[3]*NewsOne, Limbaugh: Obama and Oprah are only Successful because they're Black, written by Casey Gane-McCalla, July 7, 2010*

[4]*Business Insider, Rush Limbaugh Gets $400 Million to Rant Through 2016, Hiliary Lewis, July 2, 2008*

[5]*CBS News, Hannitizing of America, By Rome Neal, May 23, 2004*

[6]*Politico.com, "WSJ,Hannity inks $100 Million Deal", Fox News, July 21, 2008,*
http://www.politico.com/blogs/michaelcalderone/0708/WSJ_Hannity_inks_1 00_million_deal.html

[7] *Full Transcript of Glenn Beck's Keynote Speech at CPAC, February 20th, 2010, By Topher Lynch, February 22, 2010,*
http://politics.gather.com/viewArticle.action?articleId=281474978060978

[8] *The Atlasphere "Who Is Glenn Beck", Opinion Editorial by John Stossel - Jun 17, 2009, http://www.theatlasphere.com/columns/090617-stossel-glenn-beck.php*

[9, 10] *Forbes Magazine, Glenn Beck Inc. "Crying All the Way to the Bank" by Lacey Rose, April 26, 2010*
http://www.forbes.com/forbes/2010/0426/entertainment-fox-news-simon-schuster-glenn-beck-inc.html

[11]*CNN Entertainment, "The lightning-rod life of Dr. Laura", by Todd Leopold, April 20, 2010,*
http://www.cnn.com/2010/SHOWBIZ/08/18/laura.schlessinger.radio/index.ht ml

193

[12] MediaMatters for America, "FULL AUDIO: Dr. Laura Schlessinger's N-word rant", by Jeremy Holden, April 12, 2010, http://mediamatters.org/blog/201008120045

[13] DrLaura.com, (About Section), Dr. Laura, April 17, 2012, http://www.drlaura.com/g/About-Dr.-Laura/273.html

[14] Fox News, NAACP Resolution Calls on Tea Party to Repudiate 'Racist Elements' in Movement, July 14, 2010, http://www.foxnews.com/politics/2010/07/13/tea-party-preempts-racist-resolution-condemns-bigoted-naacp/#ixzz1sEzmFB00

[15] CNN, Shooting throws spotlight on state of U.S. political rhetoric, by Michael Martinez, January10, 2011, http://www.cnn.com/2011/US/01/09/arizona.shooting.rhetoric/index.html

[16] Glennbeck.com "The one thing the media can't stand to tell you about Gabrielle Giffords", January 10, 2011, http://media.glennbeck.com/content/blog/stu/?p=1201

Chapter 1: A Look at the Rush

[1] RushLimbaugh.com, About the Rush Limbaugh Show, January 10, 2011, http://webtest1.rushlimbaugh.com/home/about_the_show.guest.html

[2] Rush Limbaugh, 'The Way Things Ought to be', paperback edition pages 155-156, Pocket 1993

[3] 'How Volcanoes Work, Climate Effects of Volcanic Eruptions', San Diego State University, http://www.geology.sdsu.edu/how_volcanoes_work/climate_effects.html

[4] NYTimes.com, 'Global Warming & Climate Change', The New York Times, April 21, 2012, http://topics.nytimes.com/top/news/science/topics/globalwarming/index.html#

[5] Intech, "Global warming: Natural or man-made?", Jim Pinto, March 15, 2007, http://www.isa.org/Content/ContentGroups/News/20071/March33/Global_warming__Natural_or_man-made_.htm

[6] Examiner.com, 'Rush Limbaugh, 'Global warming, and susceptible conservatives', Jean Williams, May 12, 2009, http://www.examiner.com/article/rush-limbaugh-global-warming-and-susceptible-conservatives

[7] WashingtonPost.com, 'Rush Limbaugh On the Offensive Against Ad With Michael J. Fox', by David Montgomery, October 25, 2006,

http://www.washingtonpost.com/wp-dyn/content/article/2006/10/24/AR2006102400691.html

[8] *ABC News, 'Rush Limbaugh Mocks Chinese President Hu Jintao', by Huma Khan, January 20, 2011, http://abcnews.go.com/blogs/politics/2011/01/rush-limbaugh-mocks-chinese-president-hu-jintao/*

[9]*Examiner.com, "Oregon Rep. David Wu reprimands racist Rush Limbaugh for Hu Jintao gaffe", Michael Stone, January 21, 2011, http://www.examiner.com/article/oregon-rep-david-wu-reprimands-racist-rush-limbaugh-for-hu-jintao-gaffe*

[10] *MediaMatters For America, 'Congresswoman Judy Chu Condemns Rush Limbaugh's Comments Ridiculing Chinese Culture, President Hu Jintao' by Media Matters staff, January 20 ,2011, http://mediamatters.org/blog/201101200051*

[11] *Eater, 'Rush Limbaugh's Michelle Obama Rant was "Below the Belt", by Paula Forbes, February 23, 2011, http://eater.com/archives/2011/02/23/rush-limbaughs-michelle-obama-comments-were-below-the-belt.php*

[12] *PoliticusUSA, "Rush Limbaugh Attacks Michelle Obama For Eating Ribs", February 21, 2011, http://www.politicususa.com/limbaugh-michelle-obama-ribs/*

[13] *MediaMatters For America, "No, Rush, Michelle Obama did not call her daughters "fat", by Solange Uwimana, February 25, 2010, http://mediamatters.org/blog/201002250058*

[14] *PoliticusUSA, "Rush Limbaugh Wants The TSA To Grope Obama's 9 Year Old Daughter", November 23, 2010, http://www.politicususa.com/limbaugh-sasha-obama/*

[15] *Paul D. Colford. The Rush Limbaugh story: talent on loan from God: an unauthorized biography. New York. St. Martin's Press, 1993. ISBN 0-312-09906-1.*

[16] *Daniel Henninger, April 29, 2005 "Rush to Victory". The Wall Street Journal.*

[17] *CNN.com,' Limbaugh admits addiction to pain medication', October 10, 2003, http://articles.cnn.com/2003-10-10/entertainment/rush.limbaugh_1_wilma-cline-rush-limbaugh-inaccuracies-and-distortions?_s=PM:SHOWBIZ*

[18] *CBSNews.com, 'Rush Limbaugh Arrested On Drug Charges', March 5, 2009, http://www.cbsnews.com/2100-201_162-1561324.html*

195

[19]*Washingtonpost.com, "Rush Limbaugh Turns Himself In On Fraud Charge In Rx Drug Probe", Peter Whoriskey, April 29, 2006, http://www.washingtonpost.com/wp-dyn/content/article/2006/04/28/AR2006042801692.html*

[20] *Rush TV show, October 5, 1995, www.fair.org, (Extra! November/December 2003)*

[21] *Time.com, 'Was Rush Limbaugh right to resign from ESPN?', October 6,2003, http://www.time.com/time/nation/article/0,8599,493270,00.html*

[22] *The Seattle Times, 'Rush Limbaugh's a disloyal clown when he says he hopes Obama fails', by Leonard Pitts Jr., January 23, 2009, http://seattletimes.nwsource.com/html/opinion/2008664366_opina25pitts.html*

Chapter 2: The Hannitization of America

[1] *Hannity.com, 'Sean Hannity' April 23, 2012, http://www.hannity.com/pages/our-team*

[2]*Americanrhetoric.com,"Martin Luther King Jr.", Retrieved June 1, 2012, http://www.americanrhetoric.com/speeches/mlkihaveadream.htm*

[3,] *CBSnews.com, 'Hannitization' Of America', by Rome Neal, December 5, 2007, http://www.cbsnews.com/2100-3445_162-619045.html*

[4,5,6] *FreedomAlliance.org, April 23, 2012, http://www.freedomalliance.org/index.php?option=com_content&task=view&id=2674&Itemid=101*

[7 8,9, 10, 11, 12, 13, 14, 15, 16] *DebbieSchlussel.com, 'Sean Hannity's Freedom CONcert Scam: Almost None of Charity's $ Went to Injured Troops, Kids of Fallen Troops; G5s for Vannity?', by Debbie Schlussel, March 18, 2010, http://www.debbieschlussel.com/6938/sean-hannitys-freedom-concert-scam-only-7-of-charitys-money-went-to-injured-troops-kids-of-fallen-troops-g5s-g6s-for-vannity/*

[17] *Citizens for Responsibility and Ethics in Washington (CREW), 'CREW Files Complaints with FTC and IRS against Sean Hannity, Freedom Concerts, and Freedom Alliance' March 29, 2010, http://www.citizensforethics.org/index.php/press/entry/crew-files-complaints-with-ftc-and-irs-against-sean-hannity/*

[18] *The First Church of Free Speech, 'Sean Hannity's Concert Scam', by Jason Peppers, August 12, 2007, http://daltonator.net/durandal/blog/?p=106*

[19] *NewsCorpse.com, 'Sean Hannity's Lies Exposed By Jon Stewart', by Mark, November 11, 2009, http://www.newscorpse.com/ncWP/?p=1450*

196

[20] Politics Daily, 'Sean Hannity: 'Jon Stewart Was Right' About Swapped Demonstration Footage', http://www.politicsdaily.com/2009/11/12/sean-hannity-jon-stewart-was-right-about-swapped-video/

[21] MediaMatters.org, 'The Rush Limbaugh School Of Economics: Sean Hannity Further Improves Unemployment Rate Inherited From Bush', August 15, 2011, http://mediamatters.org/blog/201108150032

[22] USNews.com, 'January Unemployment Rate Hits 7.6 Percent: What You Need to Know', by Liz Wolgemuth, February 9, 2009, http://money.usnews.com/money/careers/articles/2009/02/06/january-unemployment-rate-hits-76-percent-what-you-need-to-know

[23, 24] War On Racism, 'Fox's Sean Hannity Confronted Over Relationship with Neo-Nazi Hal Turner', March 30.2008, http://waronracism.blogspot.com/2008_03_01_archive.html

[25] Mashpedia, Hal Turner, April 25, 2012, http://www.mashpedia.com/Hal_Turner

[26] Newsvine.com, 'Hal Turner offers to release Sean Hannity tapes for $100,000', by Cory Perry, March 29, 2008, http://coryperry.newsvine.com/_news/2008/03/29/1398872-hal-turner-offers-to-release-sean-hannity-tapes-for-100000

Chapter 3: The Confusion of Entertainment

[1] Glennbeck.com, April 25, 2012, http://www.glennbeck.com/

[2] Glennbeck.com, 'About Glenn', April 25, 2012, http://www.glennbeck.com/content/program/

[3, 4, 5] Forbes.com, 'Glenn Beck Inc.", by Lacey Rose, April 8, 2010, http://www.forbes.com/forbes/2010/0426/entertainment-fox-news-simon-schuster-glenn-beck-inc.html

[6, 7] TheBlaze.com, 'Beck & Family Harassed During Outdoor Movie Night in NYC Park', by Jonathon M. Seidl, June 28, 2011, http://www.theblaze.com/stories/beck-family-accosted-and-harassed-during-outdoor-movie-night-in-nyc-park/

[8] Politico.com, "Fox's Beck, Obama is 'a racist'", July 28, 2009, http://www.politico.com/blogs/michaelcalderone/0709/Foxs_Beck_Obama_is_a_racist.html

[9] MediaMatters For America, "Radio host Glenn Beck "thinking about killing Michael Moore", May 18, 2005, May 17 broadcast of The Glenn Beck Program, http://mediamatters.org/research/200505180008?is_gsa=1&final=1

197

[10] World911Truth.org, "Glenn Beck: I didn't think I could hate victims faster than the 9-11vicims", August 28, 2010, http://world911truth.org/glenn-beck-i-didnt-think-i-could-hate-victims-faster-than-the-911-victims/\

[11] Forbes.com, 'Glenn Beck Inc.", by Lacey Rose, April 8, 2010, http://www.forbes.com/forbes/2010/0426/entertainment-fox-news-simon-schuster-glenn-beck-inc.html

[12]Forbes.com, "Beck and Olbermann Far More Disliked Than Loved, Data Shows", Jeff Bercovici, June 8, 2011, http://www.forbes.com/sites/jeffbercovici/2011/06/08/beck-and-olbermann-far-more-hated-than-loved-data-shows/2/

[13]AncoragePess.com, "Deconstructing Glenn Beck - The author of a recent Glenn Beck biography reveals what he's learned about the conservative pundit due to speak in Anchorage on September 11", David Holthouse and Brendan Joel Kelley, September 9, 2010, http://www.anchoragepress.com/news/deconstructing-glenn-beck---the-author-of-a-recent/article_69d64a8e-3730-5cdd-8a25-be91b2662420.html

[14]CBSNes.com, "Glenn Beck: "Something Beyond Imagination is Happening", Brian Montpoli, August 28, 2010, http://www.cbsnews.com/8301-503544_162-20014986-503544.html

[15]LAtimes.com, " Conservative rally in D.C. draws thousands", |Michael A. Memoli and Kim Geiger, August 29, 2010, http://articles.latimes.com/2010/aug/29/nation/la-na-beck-rally-20100829

[16,17,18]ChicagoPressRelease.com, "Coincidence, Glenn Beck says, of rally on anniversary of King speech", August 27, 2010, http://chicagopressrelease.com/news/coincidence-glenn-beck-says-of-rally-on-anniversary-of-king-speech

[19] ABCnews.com, "Glenn Beck's "Restoring Honor" Rally Draws Thousands", Human Khan and Kevin Dolak, August 28, 2010, http://abcnews.go.com/Politics/thousands-gather-dc-becks-restoring-honor-rally/story?id=11504433

[20] Orlando Sentinel, "2 Rallies, 2 Visions for America", Michael A. Memoli and Kim Geiger, August 29, 2010, page A8

[21] 98.3 WOW-FM Radio, On Air Staff- Glenn Beck, May 1, 2012, http://983wowfm.com/showdj.asp?DJID=28727

[22] GlennBeck.com, "Amazing Prediction": Hillary Clinton for President in 2012?", August 4, 2011, http://www.glennbeck.com/2011/04/04/amazing-prediction-hillary-clinton-for-president-in-2012/

[23]The Washington Independent, "Glenn Beck at CPAC: 'Progressivism Is a Cancer in America', David Weigel, February 20, 2010,

http://washingtonindependent.com/77222/glenn-beck-at-cpac-progressivism-is-a-cancer-in-america

[24]*ProgressiveLiving.org, "The Definition of Progressivism", May 25, 2012, http://www.progressiveliving.org/progressivism_1.htm*

[25] *The Anti-Defamation League, ADL.org, "Rage Grows in America: Anti-Government Conspiracies", http://www.adl.org/special_reports/rage-grows-in-America/mainstream-media.asp*

[26]*GlennBeck.com, "Leave my family, leave people's families alone..." http://www.glennbeck.com/content/articles/article/198/41148/*

[27]*Mediamatters For America, "Glenn Beck smears Obama's 11-year-old daughter", Simon Maloy, May 28, 2010, http://mediamatters.org/blog/201005280025*

[28] *Huffingtonpost.com, "Glenn Beck Attacks President's Daughter -- Days After Insisting That Families Of Public Figures Should Not Be Attacked", Jason Linkins, May 28, 2010, Updated 5/25/2011, http://www.huffingtonpost.com/2010/05/28/glenn-beck-attacks-presid_n_593587.html*

[29] *MediaMatters For America, "Echoing Beck, Rush Limbaugh mocks Malia Obama", Oliver Willis, June 16, 2010, http://mediamatters.org/blog/201006160033*

[30] *NYtimes.com, "Host Loses Some Sponsors After an Obama Remark", Brian Stelter, August 13, 2009, http://www.nytimes.com/2009/08/14/business/media/14adco.html*

[31]*Marketwatch.com, "Advertisers deserting Fox News' Glenn Beck", William Spain, August 14, 2009, http://www.marketwatch.com/story/advertisers-deserting-fox-news-glenn-beck-2009-08-14?pagenumber=1*

[32] *CSMonitor.com, "Why is Glenn Beck leaving his Fox News show?" Linda Feldman, April 6, 2011, http://www.csmonitor.com/USA/Politics/2011/0406/Why-is-Glenn-Beck-leaving-his-Fox-News-show*

[33]*Forbes.com, "Glenn Beck Radio & TV Ratings A Mess -Prophet Of Doom Not Profiting From Doom", Rick Ungar, March 29, 2011, http://www.forbes.com/sites/rickungar/2011/03/29/glenn-beck-radio-tv-ratings-a-mess-prophet-of-doom-not-profiting-from-doom/*

[34] *CSMonitor.com, "Why is Glenn Beck leaving his Fox News show?" Linda Feldman, April 6, 2011, http://www.csmonitor.com/USA/Politics/2011/0406/Why-is-Glenn-Beck-leaving-his-Fox-News-show*

[35,36]TheDailyBeast.com, "Is Right-Wing Talk Dying?" John Avlon, February 9, 2011, http://www.thedailybeast.com/articles/2011/02/09/glenn-beck-sean-hannity-ratings-drop-right-wing-talk-is-dying.html

[37]TheBlaze.com, "About TheBlaze", May 21, 2012, http://www.theblaze.com/about/

[38, 39]TheBlaze.com, "A Message from Glenn", August 30, 2010, http://www.theblaze.com/stories/a-message-from-glenn/

[40]CSMonitor.com, "The Blaze: reviews are in on new Glenn Beck website", Gloria Goodale, August 31, 2010, http://www.csmonitor.com/USA/Elections/Vox-News/2010/0831/The-Blaze-reviews-are-in-on-new-Glenn-Beck-website

[41,42]TheBlaze.com, "Wall Street Journal: GBTV Already Has More Subscribers Than Oprah's Network Has Viewers", September 12, 2011, http://www.theblaze.com/stories/wall-street-journal-gbtv-already-has-more-subscribers-than-oprahs-network-has-viewers/

Chapter 4: The Ugly Gets Uglier

[1]Travelargue.com, "The Dr Laura Program", http://travelargue.com/tag/the/the-dr-laura-program

[2]MediaMatters.org, "FULL AUDIO: Dr. Laura Schlessinger's N-word rant", Jeremey Holden, August 12, 2010, http://mediamatters.org/blog/201008120045

[3,] NNDB.com, "Laura Schlessinger", Retrieved 12/03/2011, http://www.nndb.com/people/427/000022361/

[4]Biography.com, "Laura Schlessinger .biography", Retrieved 12/02/2011, http://www.biography.com/people/laura-schlessinger-9542197

[5]NNDB.com, "Laura Schlessinger", Retrived 12/03/2011, http://www.nndb.com/people/427/000022361/

[6]DrLaura.com, "Dr. Laura", Retrived 12/03/2011, http://www.drlaura.com/g/About-Dr.-Laura/273.html

[7]CNN.com, "The lightning-rod life of Dr. Laura", Todd Leopold, August 20, 2010, http://www.cnn.com/2010/SHOWBIZ/08/18/laura.schlessinger.radio/index.html

[8,9, 10]NNDB.com, "Laura Schlessinger", Retrieved 12/03/2011, http://www.nndb.com/people/427/000022361/

The Ugly Mouths of America!

[11]GetNetWorth.com, "Dr Laura Schlessinger Net Worth", (In Celebrities) Retrieved 1/10.2012, http://www.getnetworth.com/dr-laura-schlessinger-net-worth/

[12]NNDB.com, "Laura Schlessinger", Retrieved 12/03/2011, http://www.nndb.com/people/427/000022361/

[13]CNet.com, "Court OKs nude Dr. Laura photos", Courtney Macavinta, November 3, 1998, http://reviews.cnet.com/camcorders/?tag=hdr;brandnav

[14]NNDB.com, "Laura Schlessinger", Retrieved 12/03/2011, http://www.nndb.com/people/427/000022361/

[15]CNN.com, "The lightning-rod life of Dr. Laura", Todd Leopold, August 20, 2010, http://www.cnn.com/2010/SHOWBIZ/08/18/laura.schlessinger.radio/index.html

[16,17,18]Boortz.com, " About the Neal Boortz Show", Retrieved June 15, 2012, http://www.boortz.com/news/entertainment/personalities/boortz-bio/n8Lt/

[19, 20]Discovery.com, "Surviving Katrina- Facts About Katrina", Retrieved May 10, 2012, http://dsc.discovery.com/convergence/katrina/facts/facts.html

[21]NYTimes.com, "Hard Decisions for New Orleans", Editorial, January 14, 2006, http://www.nytimes.com/2006/01/14/opinion/14sat1.htm

[22,23,24,25]JournalofAmericanHistory.org, "An Ethnic Geography of New Orleans", Richard Campanella, Journal of American History, 94 (Dec. 2007), 704–715, http://www.journalofamericanhistory.org/projects/katrina/Campanella.html

[26,27]MediaMatters.org, "Boortz: "[P]rimary blame" for Katrina goes to "worthless parasites who lived in New Orleans", February 1, 2008, http://mediamatters.org/mmtv/200802010015

[28]Nola.com, "Rebuilding New Orleans still a priority, Obama says", Jonathan Tilove, Times-Picayune,, April 22, 2009, http://www.nola.com/politics/index.ssf/2009/08/post_1.html

[29]Thinkprogress.org, "Neal Boortz: If New Orleans Is Rebuilt, the 'Debris That Katrina Chased Out' Will Return", Brad Johnson, August 26, 2009, http://thinkprogress.org/climate/2009/08/26/174411/boortz-katrina-debris/

[30]ThinkProgress.org, "Neal Boortz: If New Orleans is rebuilt, 'the debris that Katrina chased out' will return", Brad Johnson, August 26, 2009, http://thinkprogress.org/politics/2009/08/26/57967/boortz-katrina-cleansing/

[31]MediaMatters.org, "Neal Boortz: "We Got Too Damn Many Urban Thugs, Yo ... We Need More Dead Thugs" In Atlanta", June 14, 2011, From the

June 14 edition of Cox Radio Syndication's Neal Boortz Show,
http://mediamatters.org/mmtv/201106140022

[32]*Huffingtonpost.com, "Ed Schultz: Neal Boortz, Right Wing Radio Using 'Racist And Violent Rhetoric' (video)", first posted 6/16/2011; updated 8/16/2011, http://www.huffingtonpost.com/2011/06/16/ed-schultz-neal-boortz-right-wing-radio-racist_n_878388.html*

[33]*Wsbradio.com,'Meet Neal Boortz', Retrieved May 16, 2012, http://www.wsbradio.com/s/inside/boortz/*

[34]*1041theTruth.com, "The Neal Boortz Show", Retrieved May/16, 2012, http://www.1041thetruth.com/shows/143555336.html*

[35]*Mediate.com, "Ed Schultz: 'The Level Of Open Racism By Right Wing Talkers Is Obscene', Matt Schneider, June 16, 2011, http://www.mediaite.com/tv/ed-schultz-the-level-of-open-racism-by-right-wing-talkers-is-obscene/*

[36]*Msnbc.msn.com, 'The Ed Show for Wednesday, June 15, 2011 '(transcript), http://www.msnbc.msn.com/id/43429068/ns/msnbc_tv-the_ed_show/t/ed-show-wednesday-june/*

[37]*Wabcradio.com, 'Mark Levin', Retrieved May 17, 2012, http://www.wabcradio.com/showdj.asp?DJID=12009*

[38]*Directorblue.blogspot.com, "Mark Levin's Top 50 Nicknames for Loser Politicians and MSM-ers", February 7, 2010, http://directorblue.blogspot.com/2010/02/mark-levins-top-50-nicknames-for-loser.html*

Chapter 5: It's Tea Time!

[1]*Sourcewatch.org, "The 912 Project", Retrieved May 21, 2012, http://www.sourcewatch.org/index.php?title=The_912_Project*

[2]*Newamericatoday.com, "Demonstrators in D.C. Agree on Two Things: the Military and God Are Good", Nat, August 29, 2010, http://newamericatoday.com/na/2010/08/demonstrators-in-dc-agree-on-two-things-the-military-and-god-are-good.html*

[3, 4, 5]*GQ.com, "American Grotesque", John Jeremiah Sullivan, January 2010, http://www.gq.com/news-politics/big-issues/201001/american-grotesque-john-jeremiah-sullivan-birthers*

[6]*TheWashingtonNote.com, "Grotesque Nation", Steve Clemons, December 29, 2009, http://www.thewashingtonnote.com/archives/2009/12/grotesque_natio/*

[7]*NAACP.org, "NAACP Delegates vote to Repudiate Racist Elements within the Tea Party", Retrieved January, 20, 2012,*
202

http://www.naacp.org/news/entry/naacp-delegates-vote-to-repudiate-racist-elements-within-the-tea-pary/

[8]_CNNPolitics.com, "NAACP passes resolution blasting Tea Party 'racism", Shannon Travis, July 14, 2010, http://articles.cnn.com/2010-07-14/politics/naacp.tea.party_1_tea-party-hilary-shelton-rampant-racism?_s=PM:POLITICS_

[9]_News.Yahoo.com, ""War of words between NAACP, tea party escalates", Liz Goodwin, July 16, 2010, http://news.yahoo.com/blogs/upshot/war-words-between-naacp-tea-party-escalates-175320281.html_

[10]_TheAtlantic.com, "The Tea Party's Brain", Joshua Green, Retrieved June 1, 2012, http://www.theatlantic.com/magazine/archive/2010/11/the-tea-party-8217-s-brain/8280/_

[11,12,13,14,15,16,17,18,19,20,21,22]_TNR.com.(The New Republic), "TNR Exclusive: More Selections From Ron Paul's Newsletters", James Kirchick, January 17, 2012, http://www.tnr.com/article/politics/99666/ron-paul-newsletters-part-two_

[23,24,25]_Csm.com, "'Racist newsletter' timeline: What Ron Paul has said", Mark Trumbull, Staff Writer, December 29, 2011, http://www.csmonitor.com/USA/Elections/President/2011/1229/Racist-newsletter-timeline-What-Ron-Paul-has-said_

[26]_Abcnews.go.com, "Top 8 Most Powerful Businessmen Influencing Politics", David Besnainou, November 14, 2011, http://abcnews.go.com/Politics/top-powerful-businessmen-influencing-politics/story?id=14932475_

[27]_TeaPartyPatriots.ning.com, "Gateway Grassroots Mission Statement and Core Values" (Google Document), Retrieved June 1, 2012, https://docs.google.com/document/preview?id=1CgRXQ0-nVyLq6ReLf9k4BCaeLHvC-jXhzPebvxK-AD8&pli=1_

[28,29]_TeaParty.org, "What is the Tea Party?" (About Section), Retrieved June 1, 2012, http://www.teaparty.org/about.php_

[30]_TeaPartyexpress.org, "Mission Statement" (About Section), Retrieved June 1, 2012, http://www.teapartyexpress.org/mission_

[31,]_Huffingtonpost.com, "The Tea Party Movement Is a National Embarrassment", Stuart Whatley, February 9, 2012, http://www.huffingtonpost.com/stuart-whatley/the-tea-party-movement-is_b_455883.html_

[32, 33,34,35,36,37,38]_NewYorker.com, "Covert Operations", Jane Meyer, August 30, 2010, http://www.newyorker.com/reporting/2010/08/30/100830fa_fact_mayer_

[39, 40, 41, 42]_Bloomberg.com, "Koch Brothers Flout Law Getting Richer With Secret Iran Sales", Asjylyn Loder and David Evans, October 3, 2011,_

The Ugly Mouths of America!

http://www.bloomberg.com/news/2011-10-02/koch-brothers-flout-law-getting-richer-with-secret-iran-sales.html

[43,44,45,46]NewYorker.com,"Covert Operations", Jane Meyer, August 30, 2010, http://www.newyorker.com/reporting/2010/08/30/100830fa_fact_mayer

Chapter 6: A House Divided

[1]OrlandoSentinel.com, "Muslim Woman Sues State Over Drivers License", Pedro Ruz Gutierrez and Amy Ripple, January 30, 2002, http://articles.orlandosentinel.com/2002-01-30/news/0201300347_1_state-of-florida-freeman-florida-license

[2]ACLU.org, "ACLU Asks Florida Court to Reinstate Suspended Driver's License of Muslim Woman Forced to Remove Her Face Veil", May 27, 2003, Retrieved May 16, 2012, http://www.aclu.org/religion-belief/aclu-asks-florida-court-reinstate-suspended-drivers-license-muslim-woman-forced-remo

[3]AmericanPatrol.com,"America Patrol Reference Archive", Retrieved May 17, 2012, http://www.americanpatrol.com/REFERENCE/isacrime.html

[4]Procon.org, "Should the term "illegal alien" be used to define persons in violation of immigration law?", October 20,2011, http://immigration.procon.org/view.answers.php?questionID=000757

[5]ACLU.org, "Immigration Rights: No Human Being is Illegal", Retrieved May 17, 2012, http://www.aclu.org/human-rights/immigrants-rights

[6]Publicagenda.org, "Selling a New Vision of America to the World", Andrew L. Yarrow, (PDF file), Retrieved May 19, 2012, http://www.publicagenda.org/files/pdf/Selling_a_New_Vision_of_America_to_the_World.pdf

[7]MusemTV.,The Museum of Broadcast Communications, "Vietnam on Television", Daniel Hallin, Retrieved June 1, 2012, http://www.museum.tv/eotvsection.php?entrycode=vietnamonte

[8]WashingtonPost.com, "Obama Raised Half a Billion Online", Jose Antonio Vargas, Retrieved June 1, 2012, http://voices.washingtonpost.com/44/2008/11/obama-raised-half-a-billion-on.html

[9]Politico.com, "**Rush** Limbaugh, Sean Hannity, Glenn Beck sell endorsements to conservative groups", Kenneth P. Vogel and Lucy McCalmont, June 15, 2011, http://dyn.politico.com/printstory.cfm?uuid=3A0DD68A-D5A2-4DED-A232-1546F8F1B1A9

[10]RepublicanRedefined.com, "Limbaugh, Beck, Levin, Hannity Million Dollar Deals With Heritage Foundation and Conservative Groups?" T. Christopher
204

Williams, June 15, 2011,
http://republicanredefined.com/2011/06/15/limbaugh-beck-levin-hannity-million-dollar-deals-with-heritage-foundation-and-conservative-groups/

[11]RushLimbaugh.com, "Limbaugh: I Hope Obama Fails"(The Rush Limbaugh Show, Transcript January 16, 2009, http://www.rushlimbaugh.com/daily/2009/01/16/limbaugh_i_hope_obama_fails

[12]Patrick J. Buchanan, Suicide of a Super Power, published by St. Martin Press 2011, "The End of White America" page 129

Chapter 7: Obama's America

[1]Factcheck.org, "McCain's Plane Crashes", September 5, 2008 (Updated on October 12, 2008) Retrieved June 1, 2012, http://www.factcheck.org/2008/09/mccains-plane-crashes/

[2,3]NNBD.com, "John McCain" Retrieved June 1, 2012, http://www.nndb.com/people/914/000023845/

[4]NYTimes.com, "John McCain Concession Speech", November 5, 2008 (Transcript), http://elections.nytimes.com/2008/results/president/speeches/mccain-concession-speech.html#

[5]CBSNews.com,"Obama: They Talk About Me Like a Dog", Stephanie Condon, September 7, 2010, http://www.cbsnews.com/8301-503544_162-20015684-503544.html

[6]NewsOne.com, "Continued GOP Disrespect Of Obama Is Unacceptable", NewsOne Staff, January 26, 2012, http://newsone.com/1826025/continued-gop-disrespect-of-obama-is-unacceptable/

[7]Guardian.co.uk, "Jimmy Carter: Animosity towards Barack Obama is due to racism", Ewen MacAskill, September 16, 2009, http://www.guardian.co.uk/world/2009/sep/16/jimmy-carter-racism-barack-obama

[8]Csmonitor.com, "What were two Republicans thinking, calling Obama 'tar baby' and 'boy'?", Patrik Jonsson, Staff Writer, August 3, 2011, http://www.csmonitor.com/USA/Politics/2011/0803/What-were-two-Republicans-thinking-calling-Obama-tar-baby-and-boy

[9]Csmonitor.com, "Harry Reid: racist or political realist?", Mark Sappenfield, Staff Writer, January 10, 2010, http://www.csmonitor.com/USA/2010/0110/Harry-Reid-racist-or-political-realist

[10]NYTimes.com, "Barack Obama's Inaugural Address", As transcribed by CQ Transcriptions, January 20, 2009,

The Ugly Mouths of America!

http://www.nytimes.com/2009/01/20/us/politics/20text-obama.html?pagewanted=all

[11]HistoricWords.com, "John Adams – Our Constitution Was Made Only For A Moral And Religious People", Posted by Billy Hart, Retrieved June 1, 2012, http://historicwords.com/american-history/john-adams-our-constitution-was-made-only-for-a-moral-and-religious-people/

[12]KRMG.com, "Sean Hannity| Your home for the "Stop Obama Express", Retrieved June 1, 2012, http://www.krmg.com/entertainment/personalities/shows/sean-hannity/

[13]Mediamatters.org, "Sean Hannity: Media Matters' 2008 Misinformer of the Year", December 17, 2008, Retrieved June 1, 2012, http://mediamatters.org/research/200812170007

[14]Dailykos.com, "Beck warns teabaggers: Stop Obama or face "the end of America as you know it", November 19, 2009, http://www.dailykos.com/tv/w/002356/

[15]PoliticusUSA.com, "Colin Powell Stomps a Mud Hole In Sean Hannity and Walks it Dry", Jason Easley, May 23, 2012, http://www.politicususa.com/colin-powell-sean-hannity.html

[16,17,18]NYTimes.com, "In a Generation, Minorities May Be the U.S. Majority", Sam Roberts, August 13, 2008, http://www.nytimes.com/2008/08/14/washington/14census.html?pagewanted=all

[19,20,21]PewHispanic.org, "A Portrait of Unauthorized Immigrants in the United States", Jeffrey S. Passel, Senior Demographer and D'Vera Cohn, Senior Writer, April 14, 2009, http://pewhispanic.org/files/reports/107.pdf

[22,23]Brookings.edu, "America's Diverse Future: Initial Glimpses at the U.S. Child Population from the 2010 Census", Series: State of Metropolitan America | Number 26 of 55, April 6, 2011, http://www.brookings.edu/research/papers/2011/04/06-census-diversity-frey

[24]CBSNews.com, "Census: Diversity Growing In 49 States", July2, 2010, Retrieved June 2, 2012, http://www.cbsnews.com/2100-201_162-1895117.html

[25,26,27]FareedZakaria.com, "The question isn't whether Barack Obama has been a good foreign policy President. It's whether he can be a great one", Fareed Zakaria, January 19, 2012, http://fareedzakaria.com/2012/01/19/the-strategist/

[28]CNN.com, "Bush: bin Laden 'wanted dead or alive", September 17, 2011, Retrieved May 11, 2012, http://articles.cnn.com/2001-09-17/us/bush.powell.terrorism_1_bin-qaeda-terrorist-attacks?_s=PM:US

206

[29]*LATimes.com, "Bush to Push Nuclear Deal with India", Peter Wallsten, Time Staff Writer, March 2, 2006,*
http://articles.latimes.com/2006/mar/02/world/fg-bush2

[30]*RushLimbaugh.com, "Background on the Bin Laden Op Devised by Obama All by Himself", (Transcript)Rush Limbaugh, May 2, 2011,*
http://www.rushlimbaugh.com/daily/2011/05/02/background_on_the_bin_laden_op_devised_by_obama_all_by_himself

[31]*Mediamatters.org, "Hannity: Obama Did "Almost The Opposite Of What Candidate Obama Said He Would Do", May 2, 2011 (Video- From the May 2 edition of Fox News' Hannity),*
http://mediamatters.org/mmtv/201105020015

[32]*CNN.com, "Obama administration to ratchet up hunt for bin Laden", Kelli Arena, CNN Justice Department Correspondent, November 12, 2008,*
http://articles.cnn.com/2008-11-12/politics/binladen.hunt_1_tora-bora-bin-intelligence-officials?_s=PM:POLITICS

[33, 34]*Time.com, "How the Stimulus Is Changing America", Michael Grunwald, August 26, 2010,*
http://www.time.com/time/magazine/article/0,9171,2013826,00.html

[35,36]*USAToday.com, "7 in 10 Americans say high gas prices hurt", Gary Strauss, May 17, 2011,*
http://www.usatoday.com/money/industries/energy/2011-05-16-rising-gas-prices_n.htm

[37]*HearldNews.com, "Obama: Expect little short-term relief on gas prices", Darlene Superville, Associate Press, April 6, 2011,*
http://www.heraldnews.com/news/x675823241/Obama-Expect-little-short-term-relief-on-gas-prices

[38]*Whitehouse.gov, "Remarks by the President on the Economy in Osawatomie, Kansas', Osawatomie High School, Osawatomie, Kansas, December 6, 2011, http://www.whitehouse.gov/the-press-office/2011/12/06/remarks-president-economy-osawatomie-kansas*

Chapter 8: Thoughts of Gabby

[1,2]*NYPost.com, "Sheriff: Giffords gunman may not have acted alone",Kathianne Boniello and Candice M. Giove, January 8, 2011,*
http://www.nypost.com/p/news/national/ariz_congresswoman_shot_in_head_YFTvsurRHy5OWGSRKnuK8J

[3,4]*WashingtonPost.com, "Sheriff Dupnik's criticism of political 'vitriol' resonates with public", Sandhya Somashekhar, January 9, 2011,*

The Ugly Mouths of America!

http://voices.washingtonpost.com/44/2011/01/sheriff-dupniks-criticism-of-p.html

[5,6]*Facebook.com, "Don't Get Demoralized! Get Organized! Take Back the 20!", Sarah Palin, March 23, 2010, Retrieved on May 16, 2012, http://www.facebook.com/note.php?note_id=373854973434*

[7]*HuffintonPost.com, "Rush Bails Water In Wake Of Arizona Shooting", Howard Fineman, January 10, 2011 updated May 25, 2011, http://www.huffingtonpost.com/2011/01/10/rush-bails-water-arizona_n_806912.html*

[8,9]*PoliticsDaily.com, "Rush Limbaugh: It's 'Insane' to Link Sarah Palin to Tucson Shootings", Tom Biemer, Correspondent, Retrieved June 1, 2012, http://www.politicsdaily.com/2011/01/11/rush-limbaugh-its-insane-to-link-sarah-palin-to-tucson-shoot/*

[10,11.12,13,14,15,16,17,18,19,20]*HuffingtonPost.com, "Rush Bails Water In Wake Of Arizona Shooting", Howard Fineman, January 10, 2011 updated May 25, 2011, http://www.huffingtonpost.com/2011/01/10/rush-bails-water-arizona_n_806912.html*

[21]*HuffingtonPost.com, "Glenn Beck Emails Sarah Palin About Arizona Shooting", January 10, 2011 updated May 25, 2011, Retrieved May 19, 2012, http://www.huffingtonpost.com/2011/01/10/glenn-beck-emails-sarah-p_n_806802.html*

[22]*MediaMatters.org, "In Wake Of Arizona Shooting, Beck Backs Off Claim That Obama Wants Him Dead", January 11, 2011, Retrieved June 2, 2012, http://mediamatters.org/research/201101110026*

[23]*Facebook.com, "America's Enduring Strength", Sarah Palin, January 12, 2011, http://www.facebook.com/note.php?note_id=487510653434*

[24,25]*WashingtonPost.com, "Obama's Tucson speech transcript: Full text", Washington Post Staff, January 13, 2011, http://www.washingtonpost.com/wp-dyn/content/article/2011/01/13/AR2011011301532.html*

[26]*Msnbc.msn.com, "Doctor 'actually confident' of Giffords' recovery", NBC, msnbc.com and news services, Updated January 14, 2011, Retrieved June 2, 2012, http://www.msnbc.msn.com/id/41018273/ns/health-health_care/t/doctor-actually-confident-giffords-recovery/*

Chapter 9: Outside In, the Conclusion

You can earn **huge royalties** just by telling others about this book. To learn more please visit

UglyMouths.com

Absolutely Free, No Purchase Necessary

This is a great opportunity for individuals, charities, clubs, social groups, businesses, or organizations to easily earn cash royalties.

This is <u>a limited offer,</u> so please act now!